for J[illegible]

cordially

[illegible]

8.28.85

VALLAURIS 1951
E
P F
T O Z
D E P
E C P D
E D P C F Z
D E C Z
D C O E
Turchin's R
Leslie Halliw
film g
British ant
rles Simeon
Cambridge
COME TO FLORIDA!
Why Stay North Feeling Half Dead?
YOU CAN BE BURIED beautifully in Sunny Florida for only
$49.50
No More Taxes, Food, Drinks, Races, Hotels, Night Clubs or Doctor Bills

Paul Rand: A Designer's Art

Paul Rand : A Designer's Art

Yale
University
Press

New Haven
and
London

1985

The following essays by Paul Rand are reprinted with the permission of the original publishers. Most have been updated and edited.

Thoughts on Design
Wittenborn, Schultz, Inc., 1946

Black Black Black
"Graphic Forms," *Black in the Visual Arts*
Harvard University Press, 1949

Ideas about Ideas
Industrial Design Magazine, August 1955

The Good Old "Neue Typografie"
Type Directors' Club, 1959

The Trademarks of Paul Rand
George Wittenborn, Inc., 1960

The Art of the Package, Tomorrow and Yesterday
Print Magazine, January/February, 1960

Integrity and Invention
Graphis Annual, Zurich, 1971

Politics of Design
Graphis Annual, Zurich, 1981

A Paul Rand Miscellany
Design Quarterly, 1984

Photographs have been provided by the following:
Wend Fischer, p. 2, Fred Schenk, p. 43,
Hedrich Blessing, p. 205, John H. Super, p. 219,
and Peter Johnson, who assisted the author with miscellaneous photographs.
Museum of Modern Art, *Arp,* p. 210,
Prado Museum, *Picasso,* p. 210,
National Gallery of Art, *Cézanne,* p. 231.

Designed by Paul Rand.

Typesetting by Pastore DePamphilis Rampone, Inc., New York, N.Y.
Color separations by Color Systems Graphics, Dayton, Ohio.
Printed in U.S.A. by Mossberg and Company, South Bend, Indiana

L.C. 85–50352

ISBN 0–300–03483–0

To Marion,
and in memory
of my parents, sister,
and brother

Contents

The hardest thing to see
is what is in front of your eyes.

– Goethe

The designer, engaged in the mournful business of tombstone carving, demonstrates his skills with humor and ingenuity on this eighteenth century gravemarker.

This book is a compilation of my writing that has appeared in the past – much of it in Thoughts on Design. *My interest has always been in restating the validity of those ideas which, by and large, have guided artists since the time of Polyclitus. I believe that it is only in the application of those timeless principles that one can even begin to achieve a semblance of quality in one's work. It is the continuing relevance of these ideals that I mean to emphasize, especially to those who have grown up in a world of punk and graffiti.*

Unless otherwise indicated, all illustrations shown in this book are chosen, as a matter of convenience, from my own work. It would be impossible to list all those who over the years have helped make this book a reality. I am indebted to my editors at Yale and to my wife for her assistance in typing and editing. To my friend, Mario Rampone, I owe a special debt for his infinite patience and inexhaustible supply of type proofs.

Weston, CT, December 1984

Art for Art's Sake

In 1890 Maurice Denis said: "It is well to remember that a picture – before being a battle horse, a nude woman, or some anecdote – is essentially a plane surface covered with colors, assembled in a certain order." He was saying about design what Vasari in the sixteenth century had already eloquently put into words: "Design is the animating principle of all creative processes."

Words such as design, form, beauty, plastic, aesthetic, artistic, creative, and graphic are hard to define. Each word has more than one meaning and involves subjective interpretation. The expression *graphic design* is rich in meaning but difficult to pin down. To most people design means decoration: wallpapers, fabrics, fashions, and floor coverings, and the term graphic or graphics refers to the printing industry, or to printmaking (the lesser of the so-called fine arts).

Yet the expression *graphic design* often draws a blank from many people. (The term was used by W. A. Dwiggins in a statement which first appeared in the *Boston Transcript,* August 29, 1922, as follows: "Advertising design is the only form of graphic design that gets home to everybody." Whether Dwiggins is the original source of this appellation is a matter of conjecture.)

The *Oxford English Dictionary* devotes two columns to the word *graphic(s);* among its meanings are drawing, painting, lettering, writing, etching, engraving, vivid, clear. It devotes four columns to *design:* a plan, purpose, intention, model, arrangement, decoration. This plethora of meanings is too broad and imprecise to be clear. Perhaps the term *commercial art,* once widely used, better describes the metier of a graphic designer. But it, too, is not sufficiently specific to be truly meaningful. Snobbery as well as the lack of clarity about its scope may have contributed to the term's gradual disappearance from the graphic arts scene today.

The definitions of what a designer does are equally broad and imprecise. Specifically, a graphic designer is one who creates ideas that are expressed in words and/or pictures, and generally solves problems of visual communication. Items requiring the work of a graphic designer before they can be printed or produced include: price tags, catalogues, newspapers, magazines, posters, brochures, advertisements, books, book jackets, stationery, logotypes, packaging, product nomenclature (nameplates), signs – in short, anything involving the visual manipulation of words and/or pictures.

Pisanello, medalion,
Bibliothèque Nationale, Paris

Design focuses more on conception than it does on execution. The designer's creative efforts in the form of sketches, plans, or verbal descriptions are often intended to be executed by others: typesetters, printers, papermakers, model makers. The design for a postage stamp or a tombstone may be conceived by a designer, but it cannot come to fruition without the skills of a printer or a stonecutter.

The revolution in modern painting, with its emphasis on form, on abstraction, on visual relationships, on unorthodox methods and materials, has played its part in focusing attention on the design of the total surface rather than on anecdote or subject matter. This too has contributed to the change of label from *commercial art* to *graphic design,* in which emphasis is given not to hackneyed, literal illustration but to significant form, meaningful ideas, metaphor, wit, humor, and exercises in visual perception.

"We know," says John Kouwenhoven,[1] "that where we perceive no patterns of relationship, no design, we discover no meaning." Graphic design is essentially about visual relationships – providing meaning to a mass of unrelated needs, ideas, words, and pictures. It is the designer's job to select and fit this material together – and make it interesting. "The reason," Kouwenhoven goes on to say, "apparently unrelated things become interesting when we start fitting them together.... is that the mind's characteristic employment is the discovery of meaning, the discovery of design." He says, further, "The search for design, indeed, underlies all arts and all sciences.... The root meaning of the word *art* is, significantly enough, 'to join, to fit together'...."

1. John Kouwenhoven, "Design and Chaos: The American Distrust of Art," *Half a Truth is Better than None* (Chicago and London, 1982), 208.

The ideas that have colored our way of seeing and thinking about design are built on the beliefs established at the beginning of the twentieth century. Essentially, the ideals of the art of representation were replaced by those of formal design, whether these ideas stemmed from the unorthodox visual concepts of Cézanne or Picasso, or from the equally provocative concepts of the symbolist writers and artists (Stéphane Mallarmé, Émile Bernard, Maurice Denis).

The designer's work, like any good artist's, is unique. He produces one design, one advertisement, one poster, even though his work gives birth to countless reproductions – no different from the *one painting* that is reproduced in numerous art books and catalogues. The designer who creates something entirely new is no rarer than the painter who does the same. And he, like the painter, is susceptible to the same influences: to history, to other painters and designers, to Lascaux, to Egypt, to China, or to children.

That graphic design is generally considered a minor art has more to do with posturing than it does with reality. The paucity of great art is no more prevalent among designers than it is among painters. To be sure, there is a basic difference between graphic design and painting. But that difference is one of need and does not preclude consideration of form or quality. It merely adds more stress to the normal difficulties entailed in producing original work.

In the nineteenth century Théophile Gautier (1811-1872) expressed his contempt for the utilitarian in art in such utterances as: "Nothing is truly beautiful except that which can serve for nothing.... Whatever is useful is ugly."[1] This was "art for art's sake." And when Adolf Loos, the same man who in 1908 wrote "Ornament and Crime," commented: "Art must be stripped of practical goals,"[2] he was echoing the convictions of a great many artists and art lovers. The quandary still exists today. Is it any easier to categorize the design of a Miró poster than it is to categorize a printer's device by Hans Holbein, the magnificent medals by Pisanello, an elegant magazine cover by Bonnard?

1. Théophile Gautier, Preface to *Mademoiselle Maupin* (Paris, 1835).

2. Benedetto Gravagnuolo, *Adolf Loos* (New York, 1982), 12.

Attempts to reconcile the formal and practical were made at various times in the early part of this century (circa 1921-30) by, for example, the Russian Constructivists, dedicated to a program of good design for mass consumption. They were largely responsible for the attitudes many today profess in the fields of design, painting, and sculpture and demonstrate that a special point of view is as important as a special skill in achieving distinguished work.

The flatbroom, a Shaker invention, circa 1800

The Beautiful and the Useful

"Ideals ought to aim at the transformation of reality."

–William James

Visual communications of any kind, whether persuasive or informative, from billboards to birth announcements, should be seen as the embodiment of form and function: the integration of the beautiful and the useful. Copy, art, and typography should be seen as a living entity; each element integrally related, in harmony with the whole, and essential to the execution of an idea. Like a juggler, the designer demonstrates his skills by manipulating these ingredients in a given space. Whether this space takes the form of advertisements, periodicals, books, printed forms, packages, industrial products, signs, or television billboards, the criteria are the same.

That the separation of form and function, of concept and execution, is not likely to produce objects of aesthetic value has been repeatedly demonstrated. Similarly, any system that sees aesthetics as irrelevant, that separates the artist from his product, that fragments the work of the individual, or creates by committee, or makes mincemeat of the creative process will in the long run diminish not only the product but the maker as well.

Commenting on the relationship between fine art and useful or technological art, John Dewey writes: "That many, perhaps most, of the articles and utensils made at present for use are not genuinely aesthetic happens, unfortunately, to be true. But it is true for reasons that are foreign to the relation of the 'beautiful' and 'useful' as such. Wherever conditions are such as to prevent the act of production from being an experience in which the whole creature is alive and in which he possesses his living through enjoyment, the product will lack something of being aesthetic. No matter how useful it is for special and limited ends, it will not be useful in the ultimate degree – that of contributing directly and liberally to an expanding and enriched life."[1]

1. John Dewey, "Ethereal Things," *Art as Experience* (New York, 1934), 26.

The aesthetic requirements to which Dewey refers are, it seems to me, exemplified by the Shakers, who believed that "Trifles make perfection but perfection itself is no trifle." Their religious beliefs provided the fertile soil in which beauty and utility could flourish. Their spiritual needs found expression in the design of fabrics, furniture, and utensils of great beauty. These products are documents of the simple life of the people, their asceticism, their restraint, their devotion to fine craftsmanship, and their sensitivity to proportion, space, and materials.

In the past, rarely has beauty been an end in itself. The magnificent stained glass windows of Chartres were no less utilitarian than was the Parthenon or the Pyramid of Cheops. The function of the exterior decoration of the great Gothic cathedrals was to invite entry; the rose windows inside provided the spiritual mood – a symbiosis of beauty and utility.

Shaker door latch, Pleasant Hill, Kentucky, circa 1850

The Designer's Problem

To believe that a good layout is produced merely by making a pleasing arrangement of some visual miscellany (photos, type, illustrations) is an erroneous conception of the graphic designer's function.[1] What is implied is that a problem can be solved simply by pushing things around until something happens. This obviously involves the time-consuming uncertainties of trial and error. However, since the artist works partly by instinct, a certain amount of pushing around may be necessary. But this does not imply that any systematic, unifying, repetitive idea should be avoided out of hand.

As a rule, the experienced designer does not begin with some preconceived idea. Rather, the idea is (or should be) the result of careful observation, and the design a product of that idea. In order to solve his problem effectively, the designer must necessarily go through some sort of mental process.[2] Consciously or not, he analyzes, interprets, formulates. He is aware of the technological developments in his own and kindred fields. He improvises or invents new techniques and combinations. He coordinates his material so that he may restate his problem in terms of ideas, symbols, pictures. He reinforces his symbols with appropriate accessories to achieve clarity and interest. He draws upon instinct and intuition. He considers the spectator's feelings and predilections. Briefly, the designer experiences, perceives, analyzes, organizes, symbolizes, synthesizes.

This is largely what the designer has in common with all thinking people. "According to Kant, man's knowledge is realized in the act of comparing, examining, relating, distinguishing, abstracting, deducing, demonstrating – all of which are forms of active intellectual effort."[3]

The designer is confronted, primarily, with three classes of material: a) the given – product, copy, slogan, logotype, format, media, production process; b) the formal – space, contrast, proportion, harmony, rhythm, repetition, line, mass, shape, color, weight, volume, value, texture; c) the psychological – visual perception and optical illusion problems, the spectators' instincts, intuitions, and emotions as well as the designer's own needs.

As the material furnished him is often inadequate, vague, uninteresting, or otherwise unsuitable for visual interpretation, the designer's task is to restate the problem. This may involve discarding or revising much of the given material. By analysis (breaking down of the complex material into its simplest components – the how, why, when, and where) the designer is able to begin to state the problem.

1. I use the term layout here because of its popular acceptance. I should prefer instead to use the term composition (as it is used in painting).

2. The reader may wish to refer to Wilenski, *The Modern Movement in Art* (New York, 1934), for a description of the artist's mental processes in creating a work of art.

3. Joseph Pieper, *Leisure: The Basis of Culture* (New York, 1952), 25.

This newspaper advertisement was addressed to people familiar with the Morse code. To the general public, unfamiliar with these symbols, they nevertheless served as a powerful attention-compelling device (1954).

To the executives and management of the Radio Corporation of America:

Messrs. Alexander, Anderson, Baker, Buck, Cahill, Cannon, Carter, Coe, Coffin, Dunlap, Elliott, Engstrom, Folsom, Gorin, Jolliffe, Kayes, Marek, Mills, Odorizzi, Orth, Sacks, Brig. Gen. Sarnoff, R. Sarnoff, Saxon, Seidel, Teegarden, Tuft, Watts, Weaver, Werner, Williams

Gentlemen: An important message intended expressly for your eyes is now on its way to each one of you by special messenger.

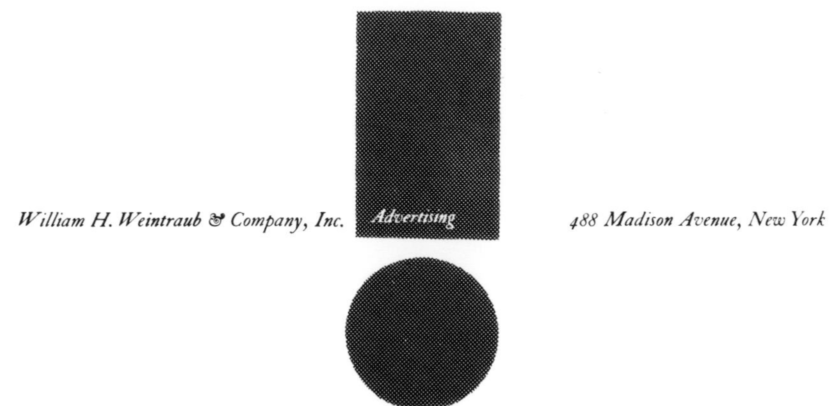

William H. Weintraub & Company, Inc. *488 Madison Avenue, New York*

Magazine cover,
Apparel Arts,
1939

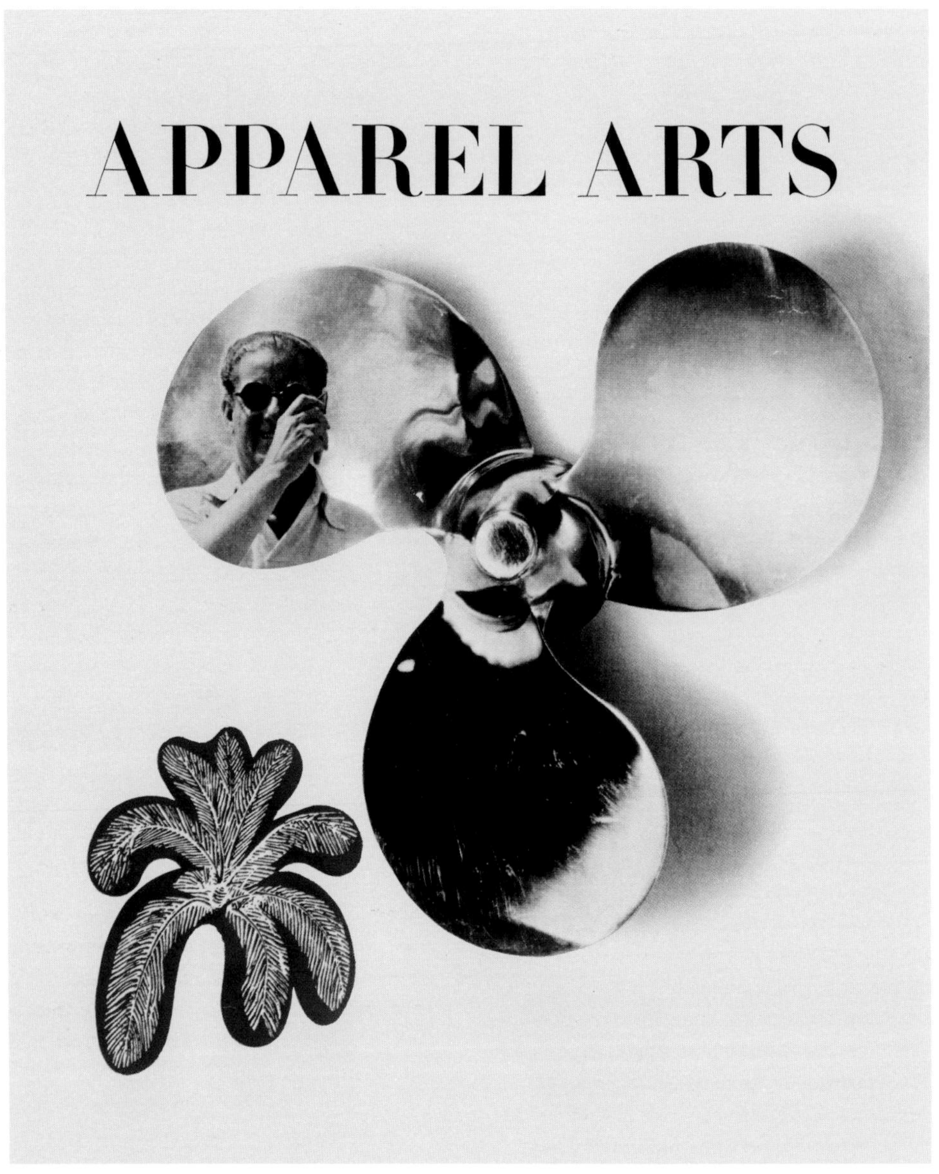

The Symbol in Visual Communication

Because graphic design, in the end, deals with the spectator, and because it is the goal of the designer to be persuasive or at least informative, it follows that the designer's problems are twofold: to anticipate the spectator's reactions and to meet his own aesthetic needs. He must therefore discover a means of communication between himself and the spectator (a condition with which the easel painter need not concern himself). The problem is not simple; its very complexity virtually dictates the solution – that is, the discovery of an image universally comprehensible, one that translates abstract ideas into concrete forms.

It is in symbolic, visual terms that the designer ultimately realizes his perceptions and experiences; and it is in a world of symbols that man lives. The symbol is thus the common language between artist and spectator. Webster defines the symbol as "that which stands for or suggests something else by reason of relationship, association, convention, or accidental but not intentional resemblance; especially, a visible sign of something invisible, as an idea, a quality or totality such as a state or a church; an emblem; as the lion is the *symbol* of courage; the cross is the *symbol* of Christianity. 'A *symbol* is a representation which does not aim at being a reproduction.' (Goblet d'Alvielle)."

The words simplified, stylized, geometric, abstract, two-dimensional, flat, non-representational, non-mimetic are commonly associated, sometimes incorrectly, with the term symbol. It is true that the depiction of most distinctive symbols does fit the image these words help to characterize visually; but it is not true that the symbol has to be simplified (etc.) in order to qualify as a symbol. The fact that some of the best symbols are simplified images merely points to the effectiveness of simplicity but not to the meaning of the word per se. In essence, it is not what it looks like but what it does that defines a symbol.

A symbol may be depicted as an abstract shape, a geometric figure, a photograph, an illustration, a letter of the alphabet, or a numeral. Thus a five-pointed star, a picture of a little dog listening to his master's voice, a steel engraving of George Washington, and the Eiffel Tower itself are all symbols.

Religious and secular institutions have clearly demonstrated the power of the symbol as a means of communication. It is significant that the crucifix, aside from its religious implications, is a demonstration of perfect form – a union of the aggressive vertical (male) and the passive horizontal (female). It is not too farfetched to infer that these formal relations have at least something to do with its endurance. Note the curious analogy between Occidental and Oriental thought in the following excerpts: Rudolf Koch, in *The Book of Signs*, comments: "In the sign of the Cross, God and earth are combined and are in harmony ...from two simple lines a complete sign has been evolved. The Cross is by far the earliest of all signs and is found everywhere, quite apart from the concepts of Christianity."[1] In the *Book of Changes* (Chou Yih) it is stated: "The fathomlessness of the male and female principles (Yang and Yin) is called God." This conception is illustrated by the t'ai chi symbol

expressing the "two regulating powers which together create all the phenomena of Nature." The essence of Chinese philosophy is revealed in the expression: "All things are produced by the action of the male and female principles."[2]

1. Rudolf Koch, *The Book of Signs* (London, 1930), 2.

2. The *I Ching* or *Book of Changes* (New York, 1950).

*Any visual image may serve
as a symbol irrespective of style,
degree of abstraction,
or relationship to the real thing.*

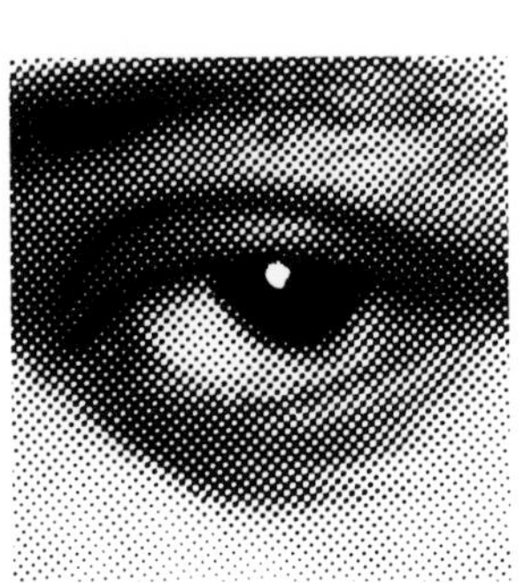

B

Here the symbol is a by-product resulting from a problem of form – that is, the opposition of the vertical and horizontal planes. At the same time it suggests the dignity and serenity of the cruciform.

Newspaper advertisement, Alfred A. Knopf, 1945

The cross on this cover is designed to suggest a pair of shears cutting up the map of Czechoslovakia. At right, miscellaneous elements: type, illustration, and trademark are unified by means of the cruciform.

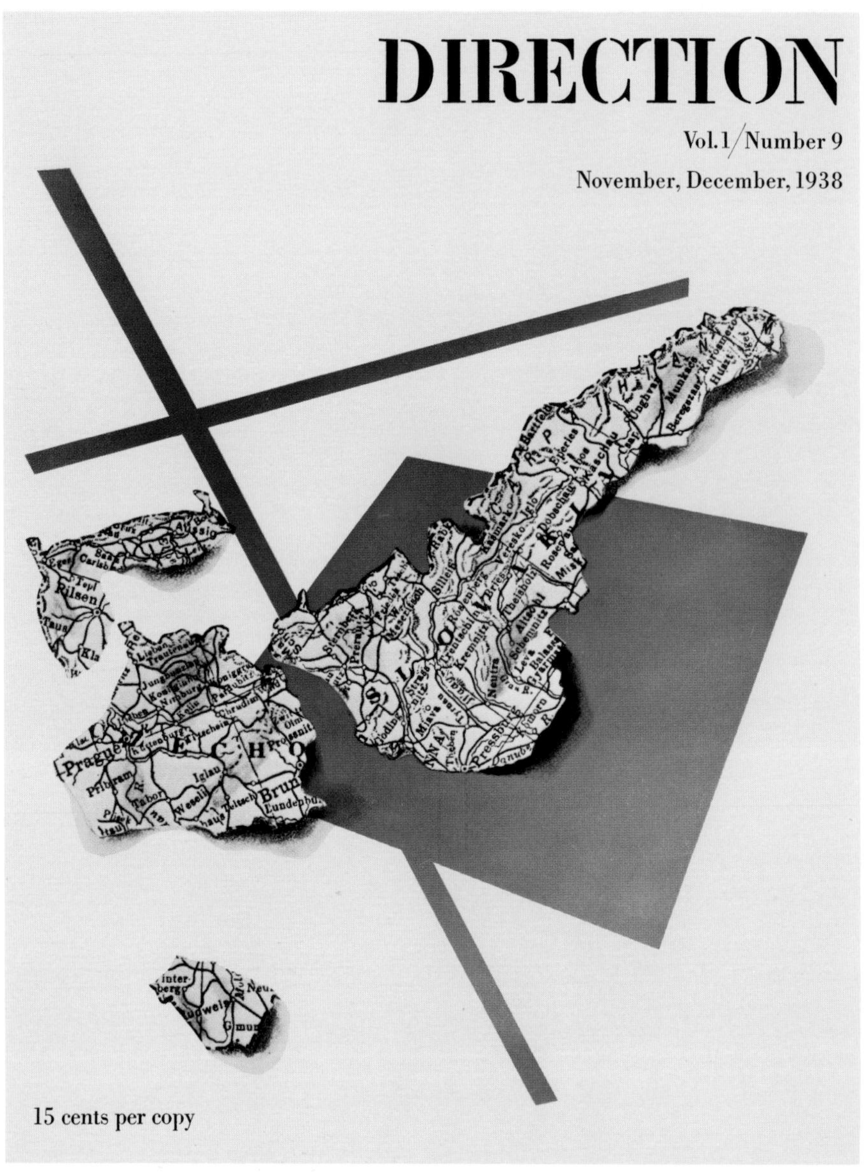

DIRECTION
Vol.1/Number 9
November, December, 1938
15 cents per copy

*Magazine cover,
Direction,
1938*

*Magazine advertisement,
Westinghouse Electric Corporation,
1961*

10,000
Traffic Signals
Controlled
by a Computer...

Imagine a computer that could solve the downtown traffic problem. This is the long-range potential of a new kind of computer invented by Westinghouse, one that could control ten thousand traffic signals, and move more cars with fewer delays. This computer "learns" by experience, tries new approaches when necessary, adapts instantly to changing problems. Right now it's at work in industry. One pilot model has been running a refinery process, not to produce the greatest number of tons, not to produce the highest profit per ton, but to produce the highest total profit for the equipment. This new-concept computer will improve the making of cement, paper, and almost anything else made by a continuous process. Compared to standard computers, the new type will be smaller, simpler, more reliable. You can be sure...if it's

Westinghouse

The symbol in this arrangement is the plus sign.

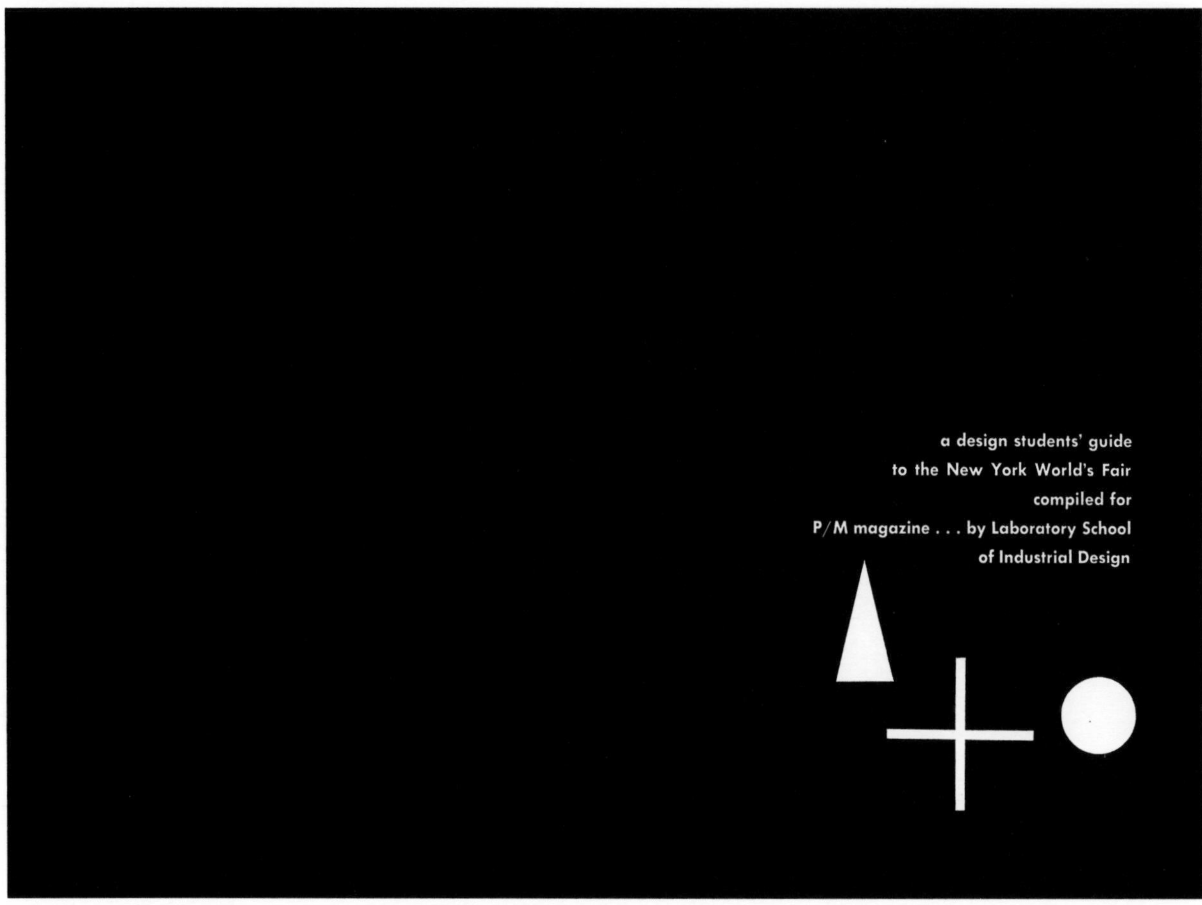

a design students' guide
to the New York World's Fair
compiled for
P/M magazine . . . by Laboratory School
of Industrial Design

*Booklet cover,
New York World's Fair,
1939*

In this illustration the form is intensified by dramatic narrative association. The literal meaning changes according to context: the formal quality remains unchanged.

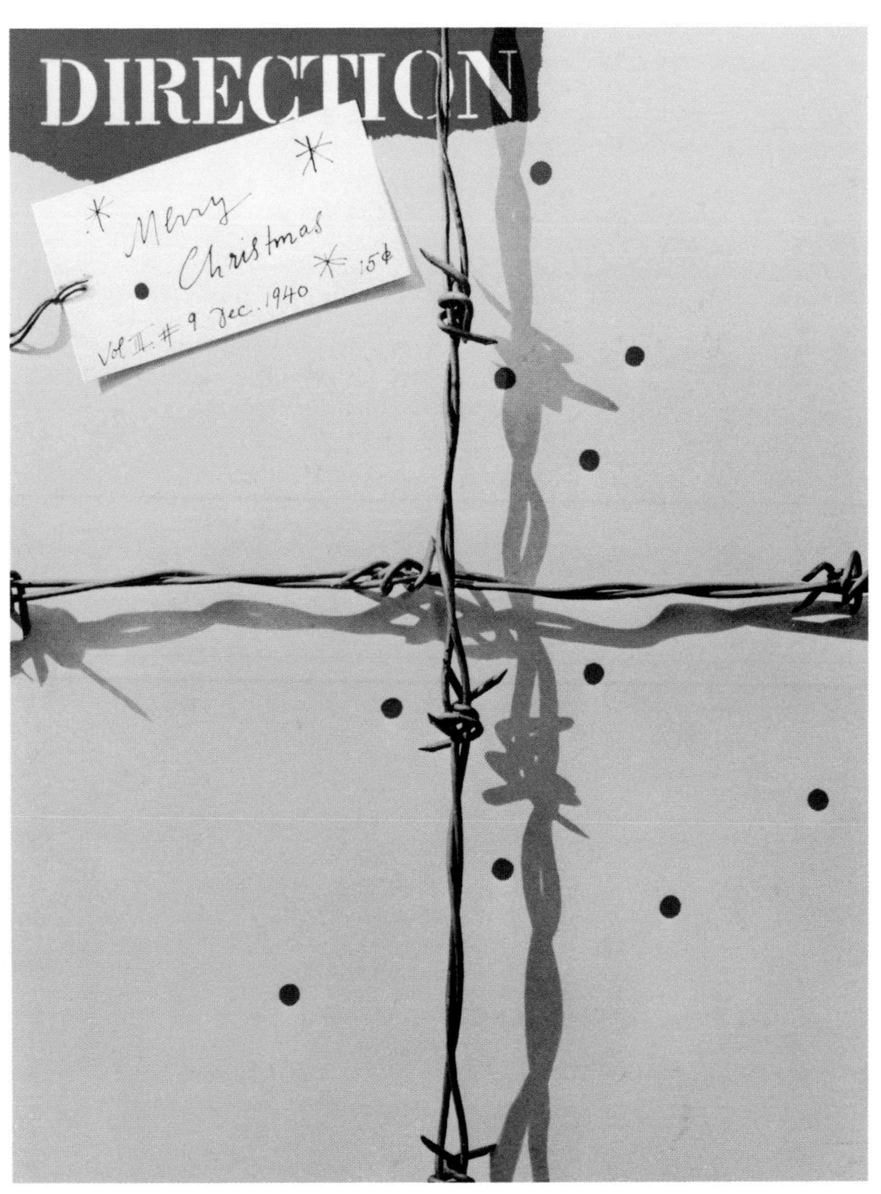

Magazine cover,
Direction,
1940

Versatility of the Symbol

The same symbol can express many different ideas. It is potentially a highly versatile device. By juxtaposition, association, and analogy the designer is able to utilize its effectiveness to fulfill a specific function.

Distinguishing between the literal and plastic meaning of forms, Ozenfant declares: "Every form has its specific mode of expression (the language of plastic) independent of its purely ideological significance (language of the sign)."[1]

1. Amédée Ozenfant, *Foundations of Modern Art* (New York, 1931), 249.

The circle as opposed to the square, for instance, as a pure form evokes a specific aesthetic sensation; ideologically it is the sign of eternity, without beginning or end. A red circle may be interpreted as the sign of the sun, the Japanese flag, a stop sign, an ice-skating rink, or a special brand of coffee... *depending on its context.*

Perfume bottle, gold wire and crystal, 1944

One-sheet poster (redrawn), N.Y. Subways Advertising Co., 1947

Brochure
IBM Corporation,
1981

Newspaper advertisement,
Frank H. Lee Co.,
1946

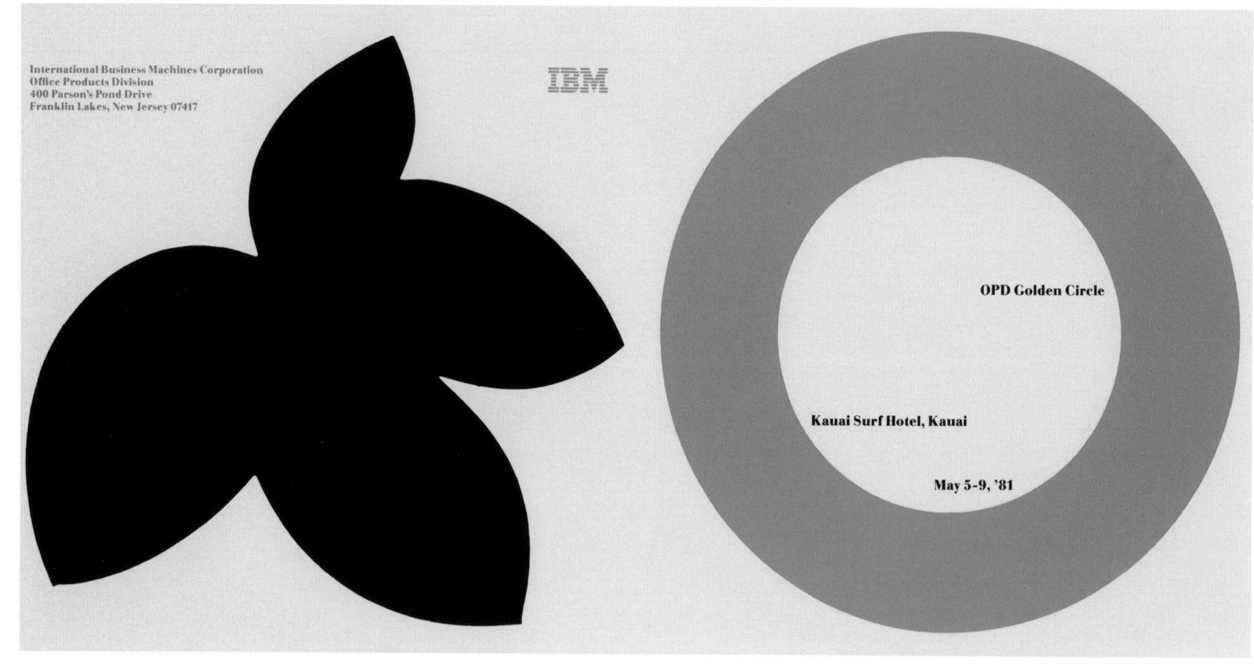

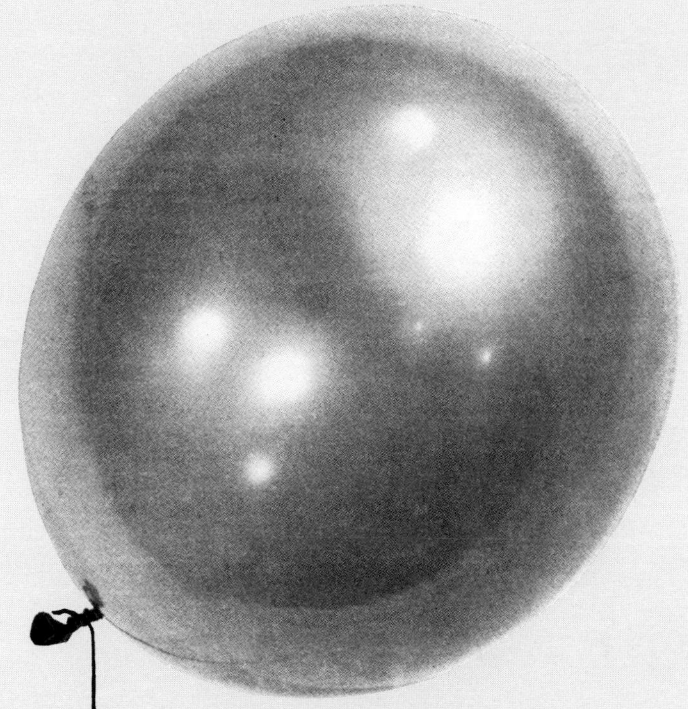

HOW ABOUT THIS INFLATION?

We are not Political Economists.
We make hats... Lee Hats.
But this we do know: There is one way to stop inflation...
perhaps the only way... that's by production.
And more production.
Not just lip-service. But by digging in, by making *more* things for *more* people.
In our case, Lee Hats... more Lee Hats.
That calls for more workers... We hired them.
That calls for more machinery... We bought it.
That calls for a larger plant... We're putting it up.
That calls for advanced methods... We have them, even to the extent of using the latest electronic developments to aid the fine old art of fine hatmaking.
We pledge ourselves to make and sell more Lee Hats in 1946
than in any year since our founding sixty years ago.
That's production... our contribution to the very
real fight against inflation.

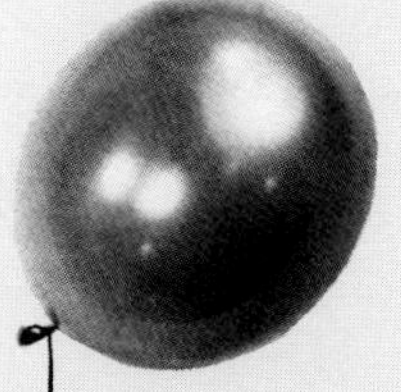

LEE HATS

358 Fifth Avenue, New York I, N.Y.
Lee Hats are styled on Fifth Avenue and made in the colorful Connecticut town of Danbury... famed for its generations of skilled hatmakers.

Brochure cover,
U.S. Navy, U.S.S. Lexington,
1959

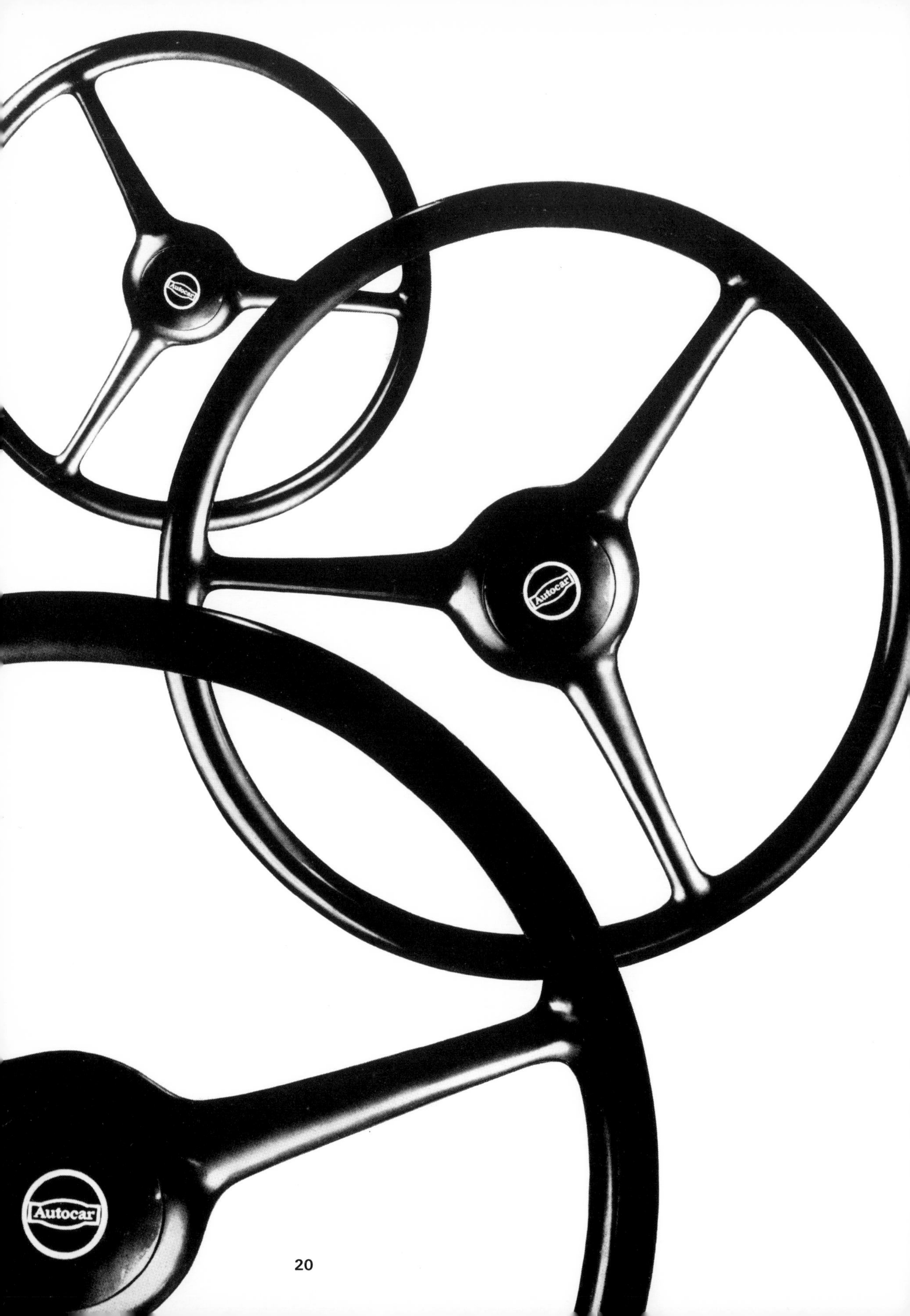
Autocar
Autocar
Autocar

Brochure,
Autocar Corporation,
1942

Poster,
Aspen Design Conference,
1982

Brochure,
Coordinator Inter American Affairs,
1943

Poster,
Aspen Design Conference,
1966

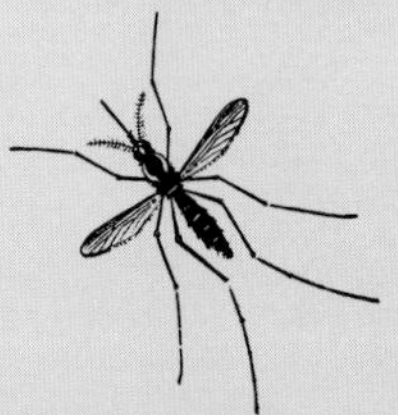

Os aviões de combate japoneses tem esta peculiaridade: o seu motor é blindado, mas a cabina do piloto não o é.

Porque, segundo a ideologia japonesa, a máquina é mais preciosa que a vida humana.

Os nazis, de outro lado, sacrificam seus proprios anciãos, seus enfermos incuraveis e seus dementes. Tal gente lhes serve de obstáculo. Defendem tambem que quem quer que não pertença às "raças superiores" nasceu para escravidão e extermínio. Assim sendo, a vacina contra a febre amarela e a tifoide deveria ser inoculada apenas em corpos de alemães, italianos, ou japoneses.

No Novo Mundo nossa concepção de humanidade é diferente.

Em nossa opinião, um ser humano vale mais que uma máquina, mais que uma fábrica inteira!

Segundo nosso código, a vida é para ser vivida . . . em paz, livremente e com saude. A velhice tem direito a abrigo; os enfermos, a tratamento; os dementes, pelo menos a proteção e piedade.

A nosso ver, o inimigo não é o homem de outra raça. O inimigo se personifica na malária, na fome, na falta de comunicações, na ignorancia e na miséria.

Entre o ponto de vista dos nazis e o nosso — qual é o verdadeiro?

The Trademark

A trademark
is a picture.
It is a symbol
a sign
an emblem
an escutcheon
...an image.

There are
good symbols...
like the cross.
There are
others...
like the swastika.
Their meanings
are taken
from reality.

Symbols
are a duality.
They take on
meaning
from causes
...good or bad.
And they give
meaning
to causes
...good or bad.

The flag
is a symbol
of a country.
The cross
is a symbol
of a religion.

The swastika
was a symbol
of good luck
until
its meaning
was changed.

The vitality
of a symbol
comes
from effective
dissemination...
by the state
by the community
by the church
by the corporation.
It needs
attending
to get
attention.

The trademark
is a symbol
of a corporation.
It is not
a sign of
quality...
it is a sign of
the quality.

The trademark
for Chanel
smells
as good as
the perfume
it stands for.
This
is the blending
of form
and content.

Trademarks
are animate
inanimate
organic
geometric.
They are letters
ideograms
monograms
colors
things.
Ideally
they do not
illustrate
they indicate
...not
represent
but suggest...
and are stated
with brevity
and wit.

A trademark
is created
by a designer
but *made*
by a corporation.

A trademark
is a picture
an image...
the image
of a corporation.

*Magazine advertisement,
Westinghouse Electric Corporation,
1963*

Atomic Power... and the race to outer space If man is to reach the other planets... and get back to Earth...he has three immediate choices: (1) A conventional rocket, many times the size of anything now existing. (2) A rendezvous in orbit, where the spaceship would be assembled. (3) An atomic-powered rocket ship. Because atomic power's efficiency is the highest, many experts believe the practical choice for space exploration is an atomic rocket engine.

Westinghouse and Aerojet General are now working with AEC's Los Alamos Scientific Laboratory to design such an engine. This industry-government team is working under the direction of the Joint Space Nuclear Propulsion Office of the AEC and NASA. You can be sure...if it's Westinghouse

T.V. Billboard,
Westinghouse Electric Corporation,
1961

Newspaper advertisement,
Westinghouse Electric Corporation,
1968

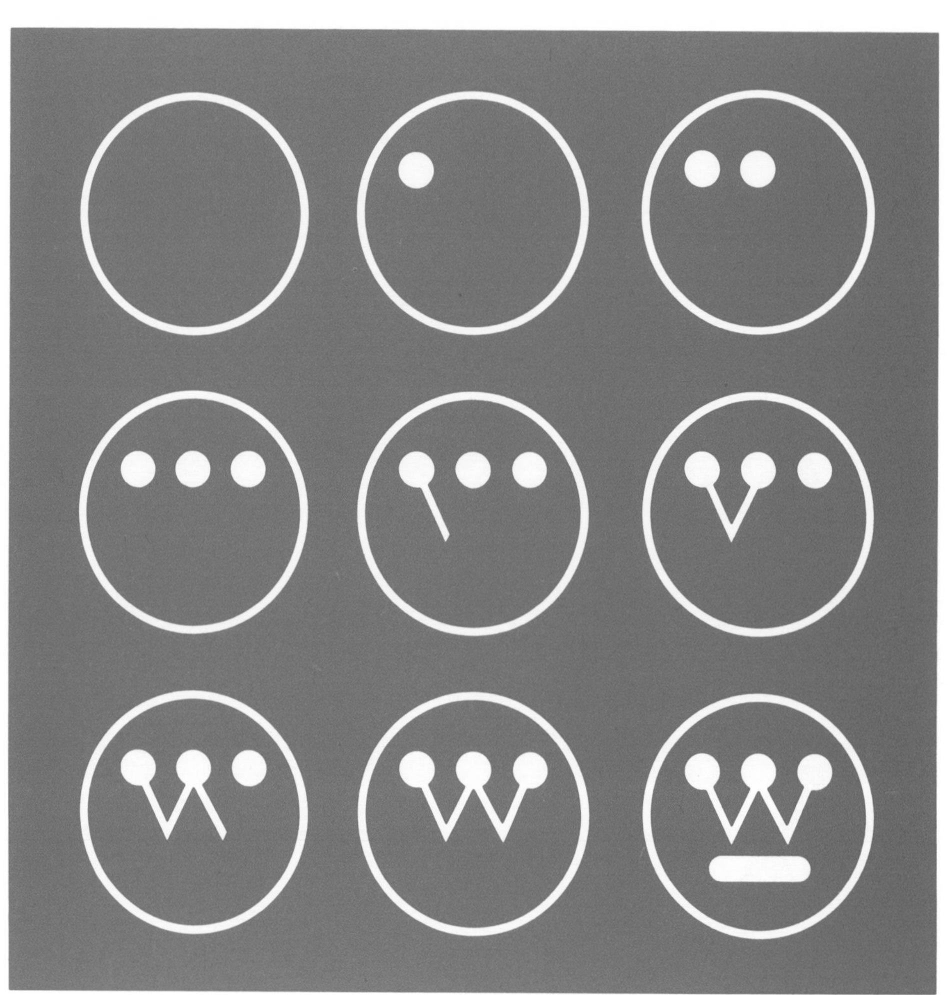

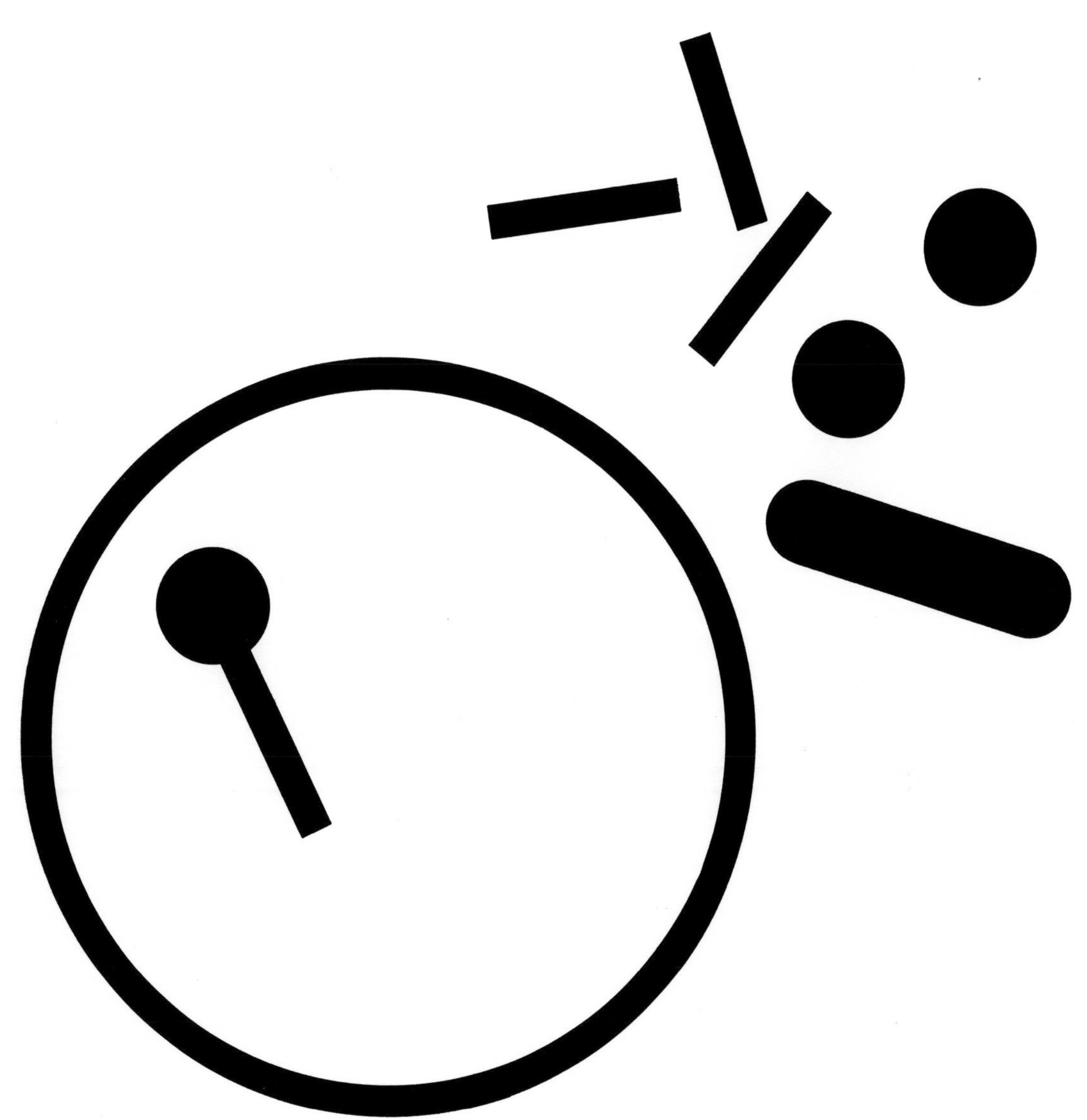

The symbol for Westinghouse (1960) as it appears today is an adaptation of an earlier trademark. The problem was to transform an existing lackluster emblem, consisting of a circle, a W, and an underscore, into something unique. Updating and modernization were a byproduct and not the focus of this program. The final design, which comprises a circle, a series of dots, and lines, was intended to suggest a printed circuit. One of the comments this design evoked when it was being presented was that it resembled a mask. Although this idea was never intended, I believe that the effectiveness of this symbol is due partly to its anthropomorphism.

The mask, since recorded history, has served many functions: to disguise, to pique, to simulate, to enhance, to identify, or simply to entertain. Not unlike the mask, the trademark is a potent and succinct means of communication – for good or for evil.

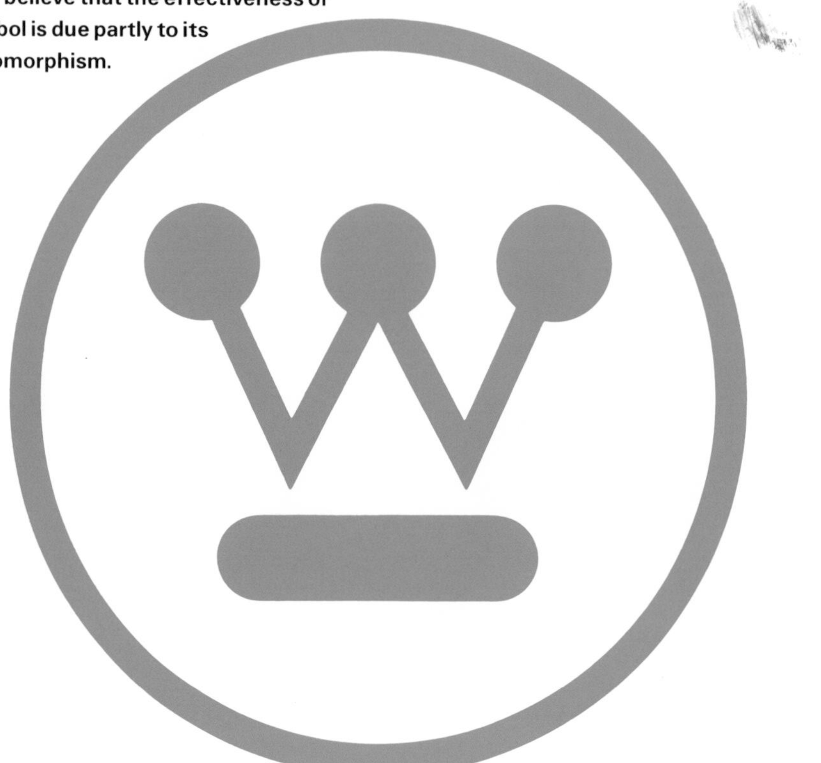

Like all such artifacts, the corn mask shown here serves a ceremonial as well as a practical function. These braided corn masks were worn at agricultural festivals of the Iroquois.

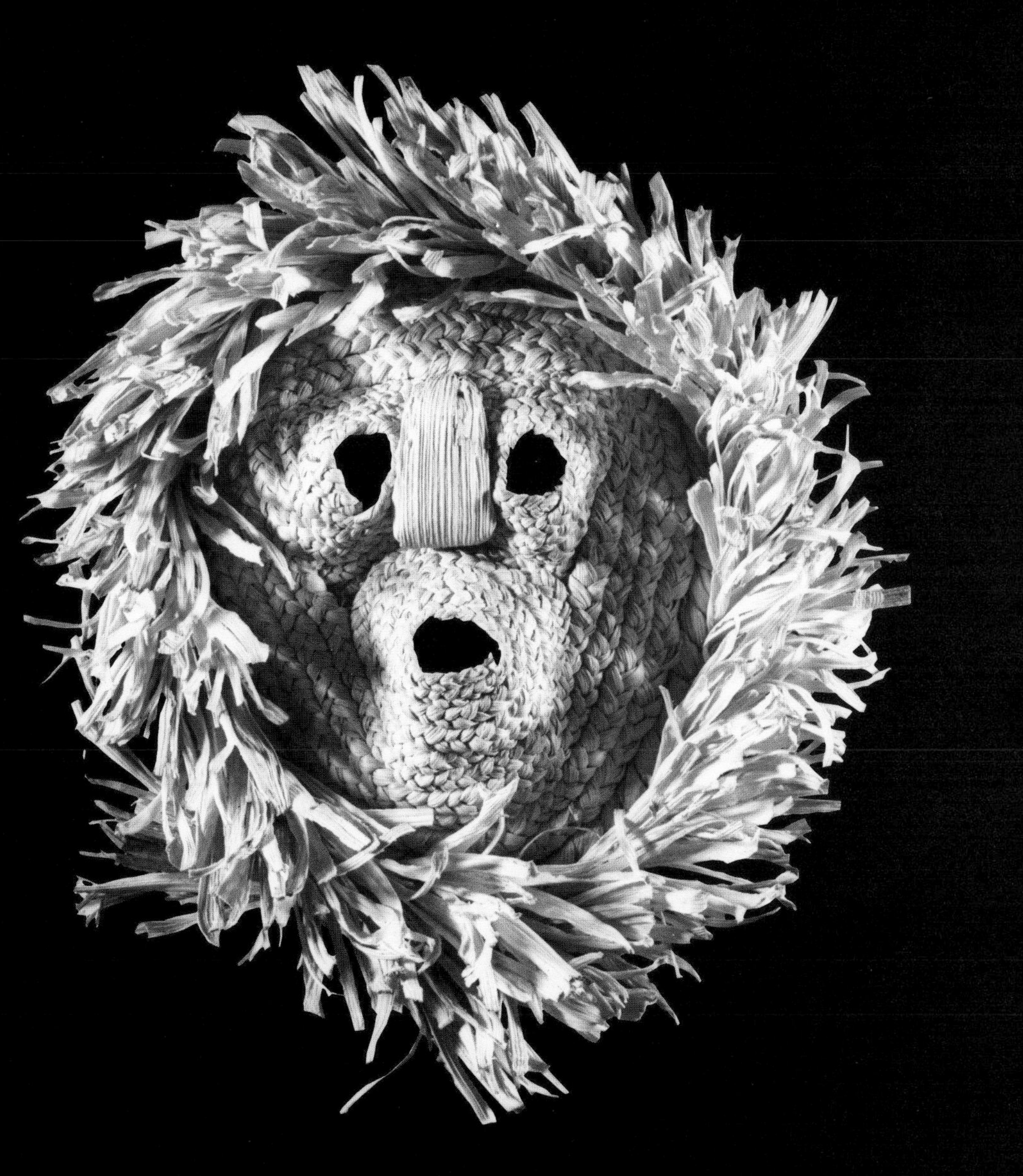

Trademark,
Helbros Watch Company,
1944

Trademark
Consolidated Cigar Company,
1959

Trademark,
Colorforms,
1959

Trademark,
United Parcel Service,
1961

ups

The need for simplicity is demonstrated in the blurred image of the ABC trademark. How far out of focus can an image be and still be recognized? A trademark, which is subject to an infinite number of uses, abuses, and variations, whether for competitive purposes or for reasons of "self-expression," cannot survive unless it is designed with utmost simplicity and restraint – keeping in mind that seldom is a trademark favored with more than a glance. Simplicity implies not only an aesthetic ideal, but a meaningful idea, either of content or form, that can be easily recalled.

Trademark,
American Broadcasting Company,
1962

Trademark,
Tipton Lakes Corporation,
1980

Annual Report cover,
Cummins Engine Company,
1979

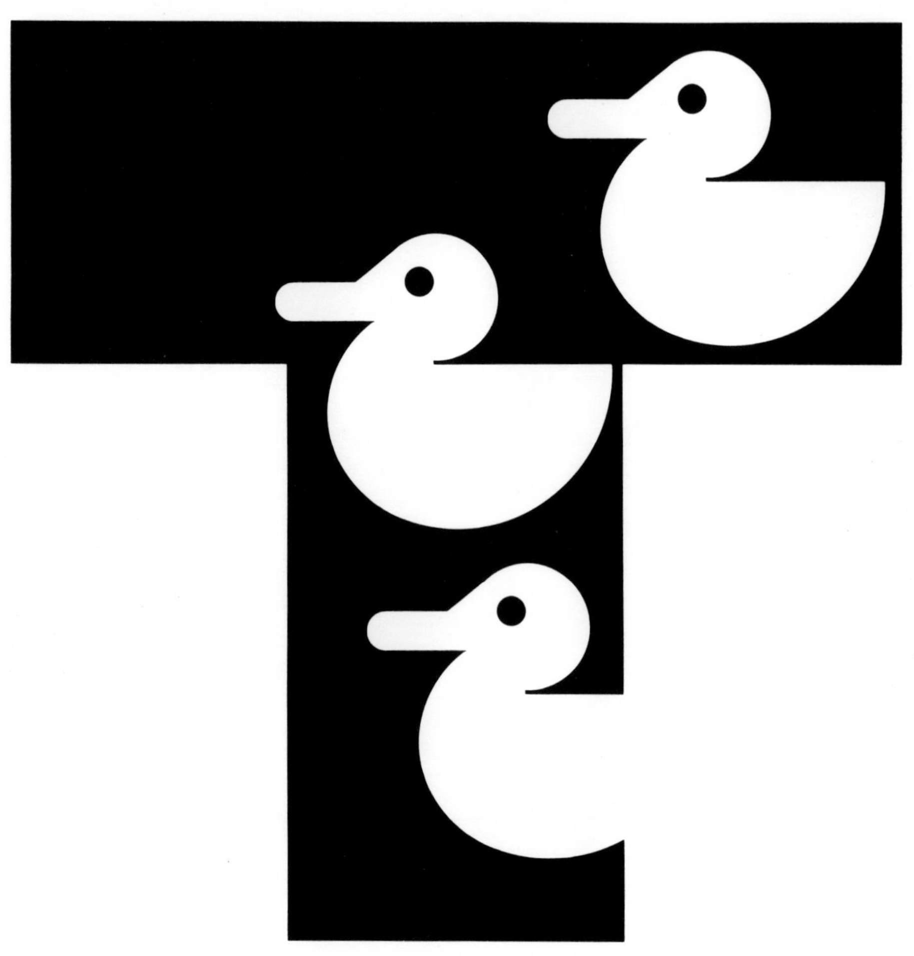

Cummins
Annual
Report
'79

Seeing Stripes

Nature has striped the zebra. Man has striped his flags and awnings, ties and shirts. For the typographer, stripes are rules; for the architect they are a means of creating optical illusions. Stripes are dazzling, sometimes hypnotic, usually happy. They are universal. They have adorned the walls of houses, churches, and mosques. Stripes attract attention.

Cover design, PM Magazine, 1938

The Graphic art of Paul Rand

Poster,
IBM Gallery,
1970

Jacket design,
Paul Theobold and Company,
1952

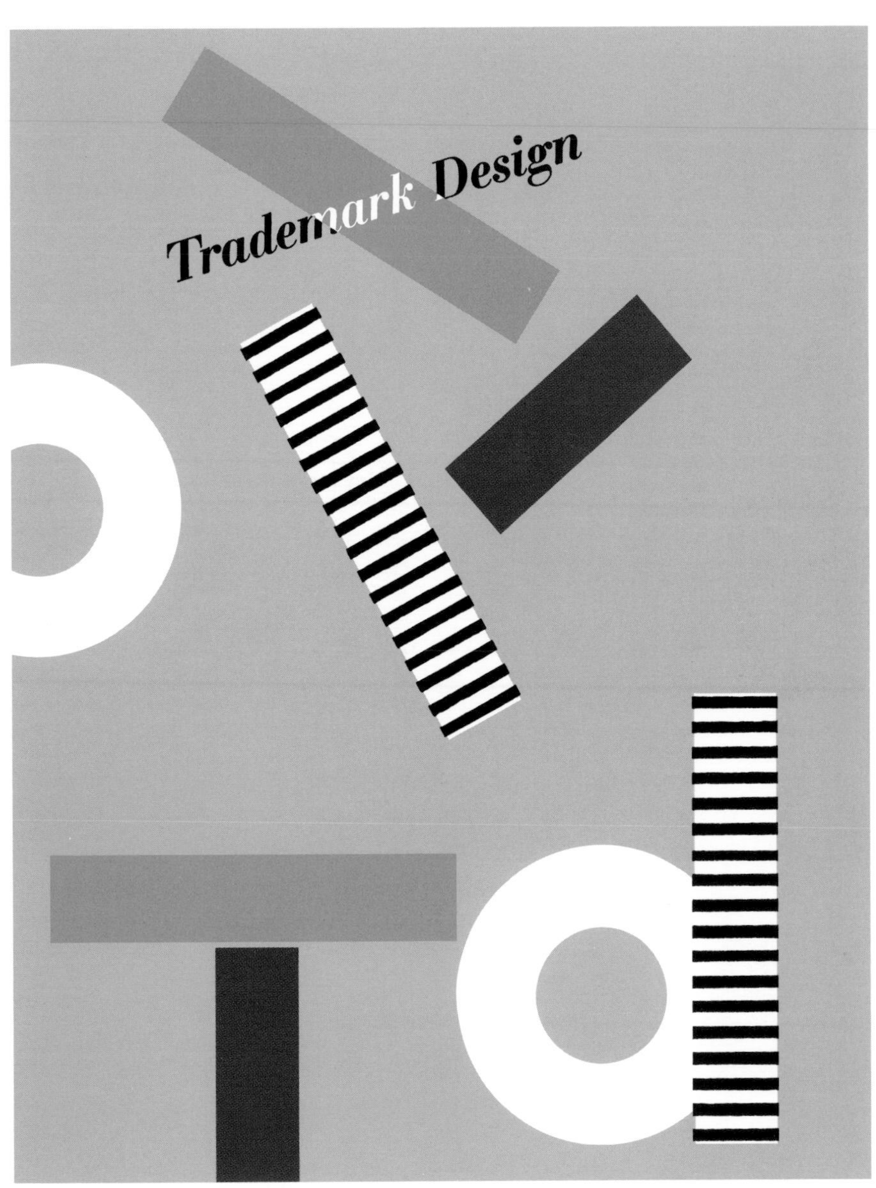

The stripes of the IBM logo serve primarily as an attention getting device. They take commonplace letters out of the realm of the ordinary. They are memorable. They suggest efficiency and speed. The recent spate of striped logos in the marketplace attests to their effectiveness.

Visually, stripes superimposed on a cluster of letters tend to tie them together. This is especially useful for complex groupings such as the letters IBM, in which each character gets progressively wider, thereby creating a somewhat uncomfortable, open-ended sequence.

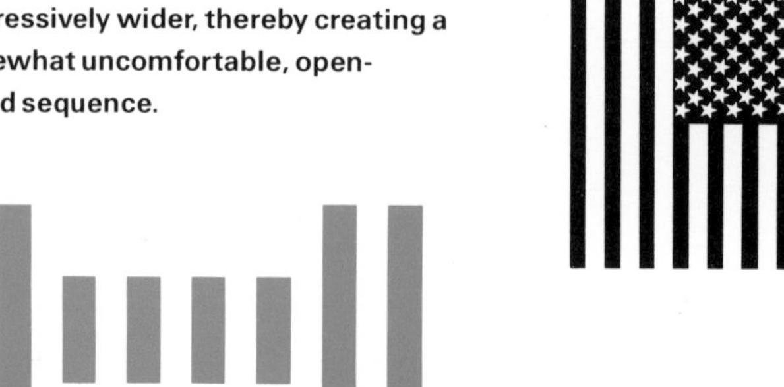

IBM

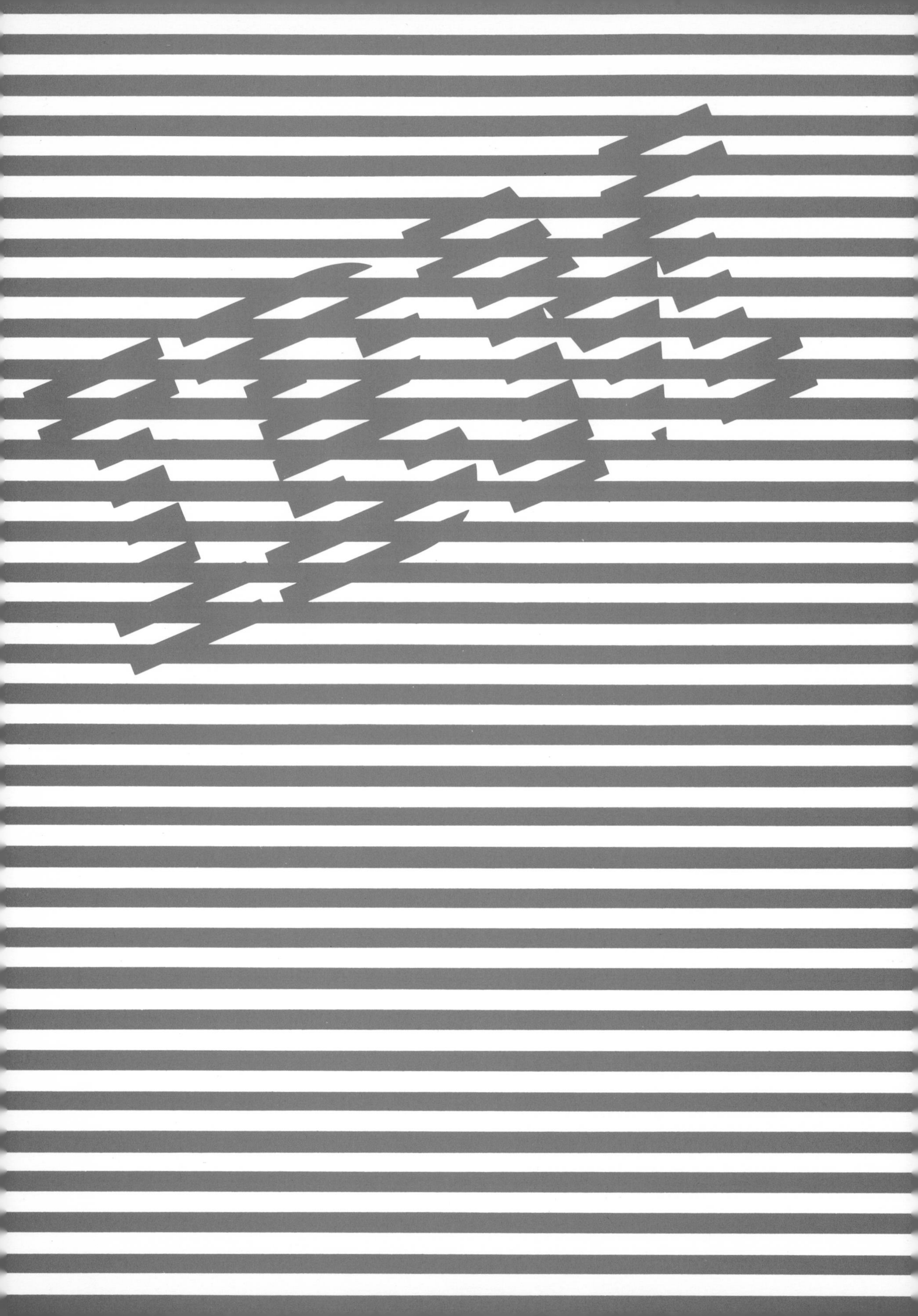

Imagination and the Image

Trite ideas, or unimaginative translation of those ideas, are often the result not of poor subject matter but of poor interpretation of a problem. In the absence of a fresh visual solution, subject matter sometimes becomes the scapegoat. Such difficulties may arise if a) the designer has interpreted a trite idea with a commonplace image; b) he has failed to resolve the problem of integrating form and content; or c) he has failed to interpret the problem as a two-dimensional organization in a given space. He has thus deprived his visual image of the potential to suggest, perhaps, more than the eye can see.

Originality and Subject Matter

Ideas do not need to be esoteric to be original or exciting. As H. L. Mencken says of Shaw's plays, "The roots of each one of them are in platitude; the roots of *every* effective stage play are in platitude." And when he asks why Shaw is able to "kick up such a pother," he answers, "For the simplest of reasons. Because he practices with great zest and skill the fine art of exhibiting the obvious in unexpected and terrifying lights."[1] From Impressionism to Pop Art, the commonplace and even the comic strip have become ingredients for the artist's caldron. What Cezanne did with apples, Picasso with guitars, Léger with machines, Schwitters with rubbish, and Duchamp with urinals makes it clear that revelation does not depend upon grandiose concepts. The problem of the artist is to defamiliarize the ordinary.

H. L. Mencken, *Prejudices: A Selection* (New York, 1958), 27, 28.

Folder, IBM Corporation, 1973

*Magazine advertisement,
Westinghouse Electric Corporation,
1962*

*Bulb packaging,
Westinghouse Electric Corporation,
1968*

Fresh water and electricity...from one super-factory

Imagine a modern factory that can produce 500,000 kilowatts of electric power—and at the same time take water from the sea and make it drinkable at the rate of 50 million gallons a day. That's enough power and water for a population of half a million.

No such super-factory exists anywhere in the world. Not yet. But Westinghouse is building a small-scale version of the system for an electric utility in the Canary Islands. Waste heat from the electric power turbines will convert sea water to fresh by a flash distillation process, providing abundant electricity and water for industry, agriculture and home uses. And at a lower cost than now exists in many parts of the world.

Westinghouse can build large or small sea water super-factories for electric utilities in any coastal area. And as research continues, scientists may find a practical way to harvest chemicals from sea water in the same process. You can be sure . . . if it's Westinghouse.

We never forget how much you rely on Westinghouse.

If artistic quality depended on exalted subject matter, the commercial artist, as well as the advertising agency and advertiser, would be in a bad way. For years I have worked with light bulb manufacturers, cigar makers, distillers, and others whose products are not visually unusual. A light bulb is almost as commonplace as an apple, but if I fail to make a package or an advertisement for light bulbs that is lively and original, it will not be the light bulb that is at fault.

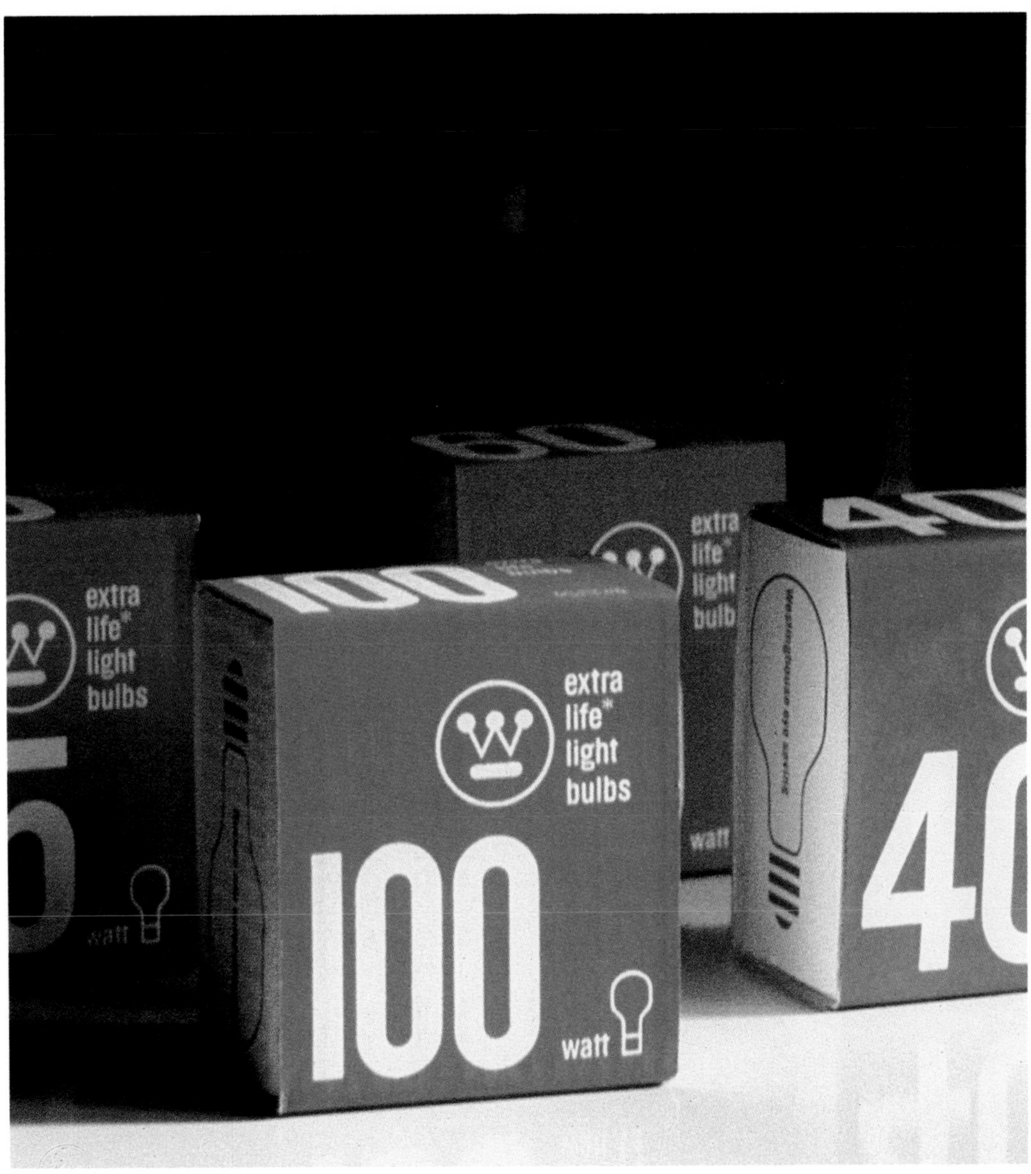

Integrating Form and Content

Roger Fry, commenting on the problem of integrating representational and formal elements, states: "This may, perhaps, give us a hint as to the nature of such combinations of two arts, namely, that cooperation is most possible where neither of them is pushed to the fullest possibilities of expression, where in both a certain freedom is left to the imagination, where we are moved rather by suggestion than statement."[2]

2. Roger Fry, "Some Questions in Esthetics," *Transformations* (London, 1926), 24.

Visual statements such as illustrations which do not involve aesthetic judgment and which are merely literal descriptions of reality can be neither intellectually stimulating nor visually distinctive. By the same token, the indiscriminate use of typefaces, geometric patterns, and abstract shapes (hand or computer generated) is self-defeating when they function merely as a vehicle for self-expression. The visual statement, on the other hand, that seeks to express the essence of an idea, and that is based on function, fantasy, and analytic judgment, is likely to be not only unique but meaningful and memorable as well.

In practice, when a design is submitted for approval, it is prettied up with mat and cellophane and judged as an isolated fragment. Under such conditions, and in the absence of competition, the purely conventional type of illustration may seem quite effective. However, for an advertisement to hold its own in a competitive race, the designer must steer clear of visual clichés by some unexpected interpretation of the commonplace. He does this partly by simplifying, by abstracting, by symbolizing. If the resulting visual image is in any way ambiguous, it may be supplemented by one that is more clearly recognizable.

In the examples that follow, the abstract, geometric forms (attention-arresting devices) tend to dominate, while the representational images play a supporting role. The complementary relationship between these two types of images is dramatized when human expression is introduced.

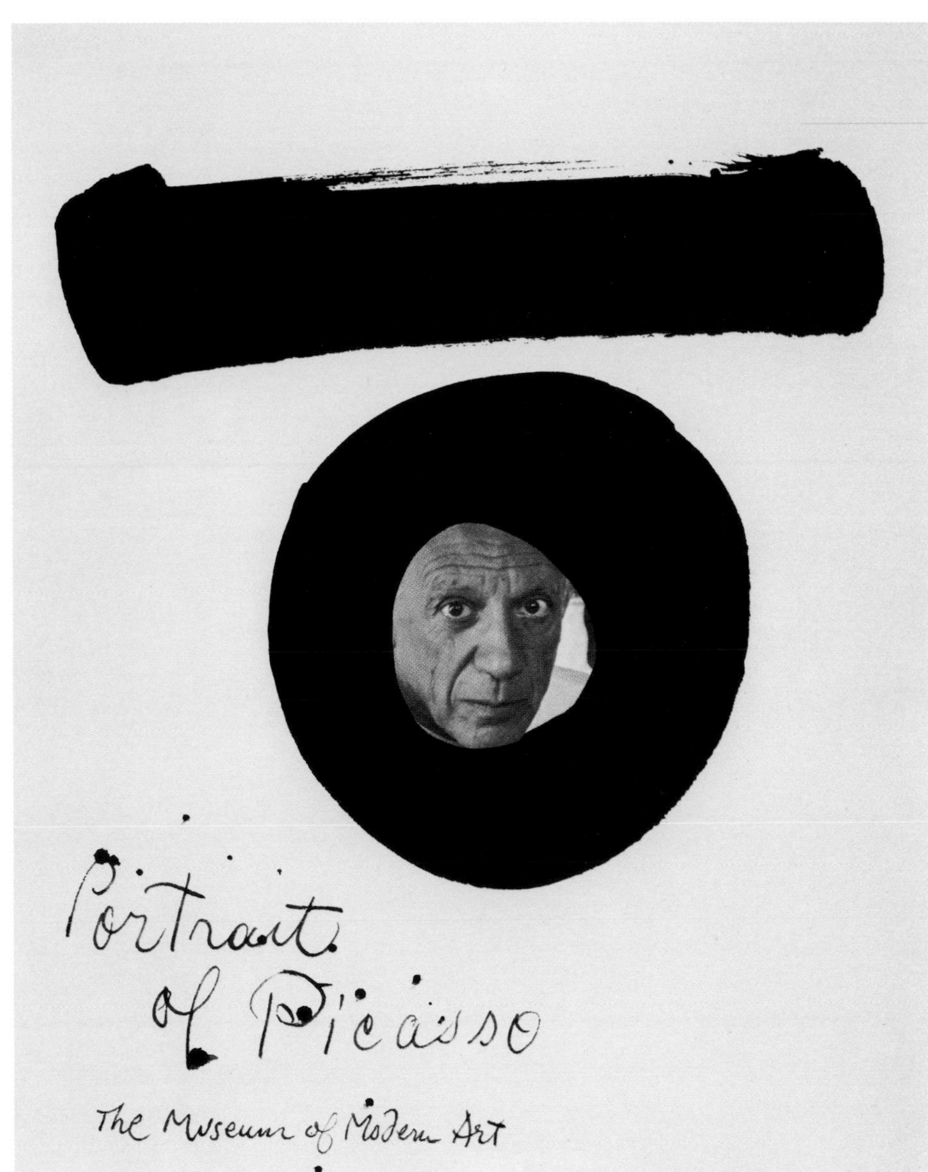

Catalogue cover, Museum of Modern Art, 1957

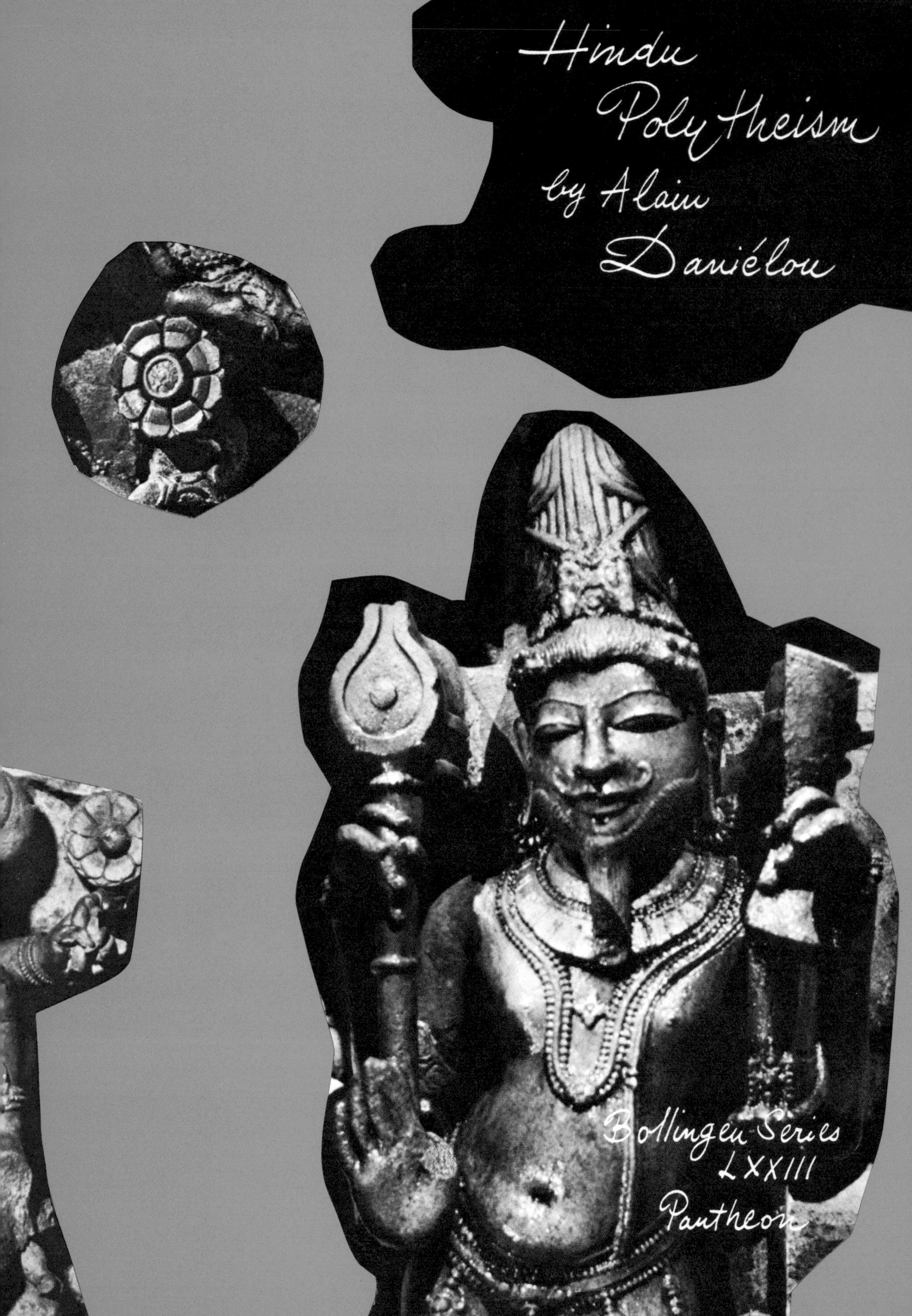
Hindu
Polytheism
by Alain
Daniélou
Bollingen Series
LXXIII
Pantheon

Jacket design,
Pantheon,
1964

Cover design,
Vintage Books,
1958

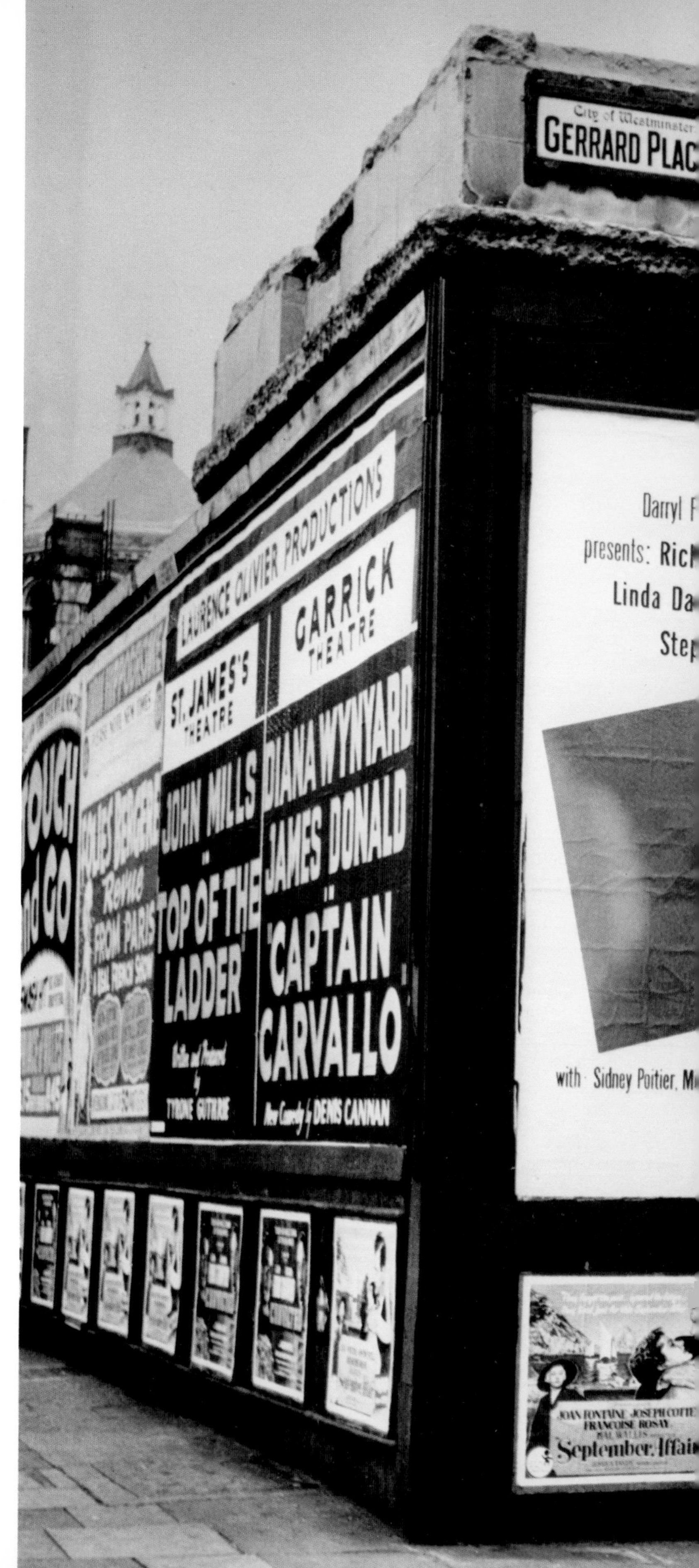

24-sheet poster,
Twentieth Century Fox,
1950

way
out
Harry Bellaver, Stanley Ridges, Dots Johnson
produced by Darryl F. Zanuck... directed by Joseph L. Mankiewicz
written by Joseph L. Mankiewicz and Lesser Samuels
20
A T

JOAN FONTAINE JOSEPH COTTEN
FRANCOISE ROSAY
HAL WALLIS
September Affair
PLAZA

TOUCH-AS-NAILS DRAMA
OF THE BIG HOUSE!
GLENN FORD
BRODERICK CRAWFORD
CONVICTED

September Affair
PLAZA

September Affair
PLAZA

Annual Report cover,
Westinghouse Electric Corporation,
1971

Magazine advertisement,
Jacqueline Cochran,
1946

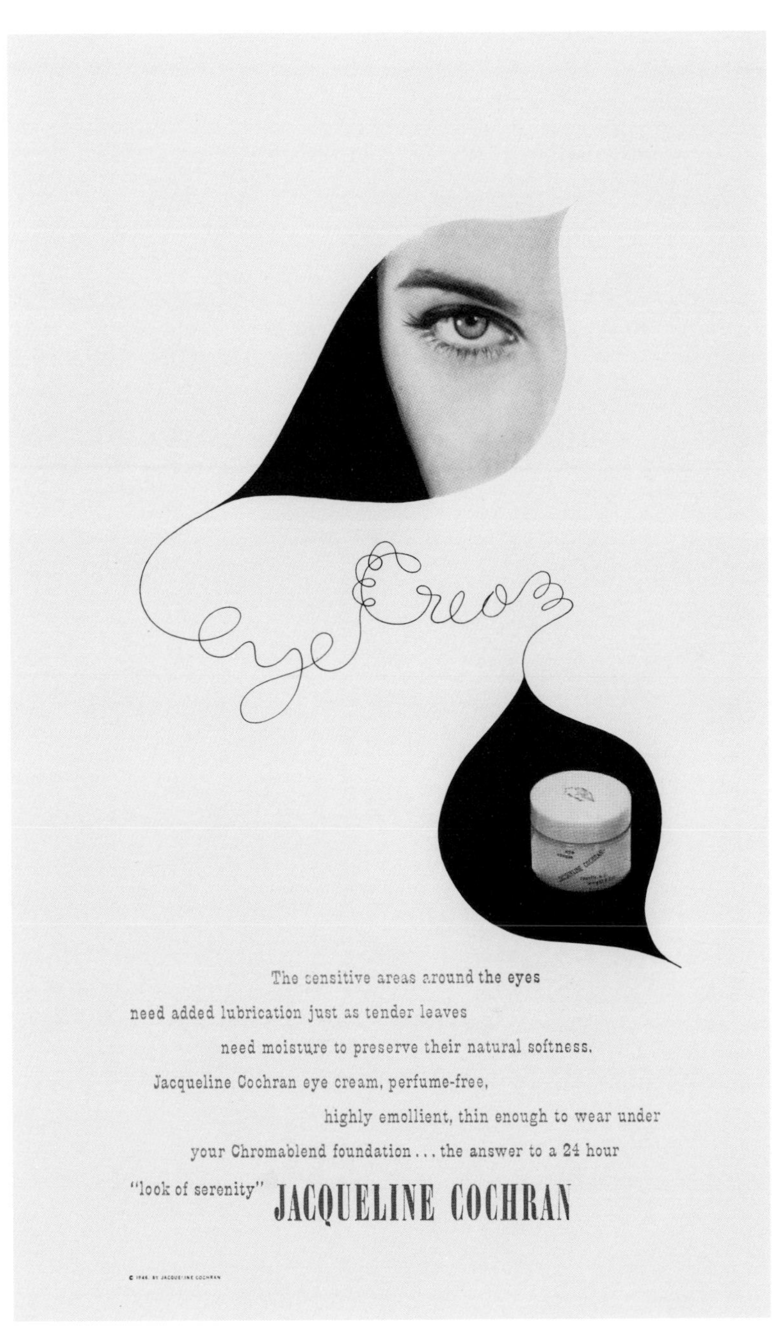

Newspaper advertisement,
Frank H. Lee Company,
1947

Jacket design,
Pantheon,
1963

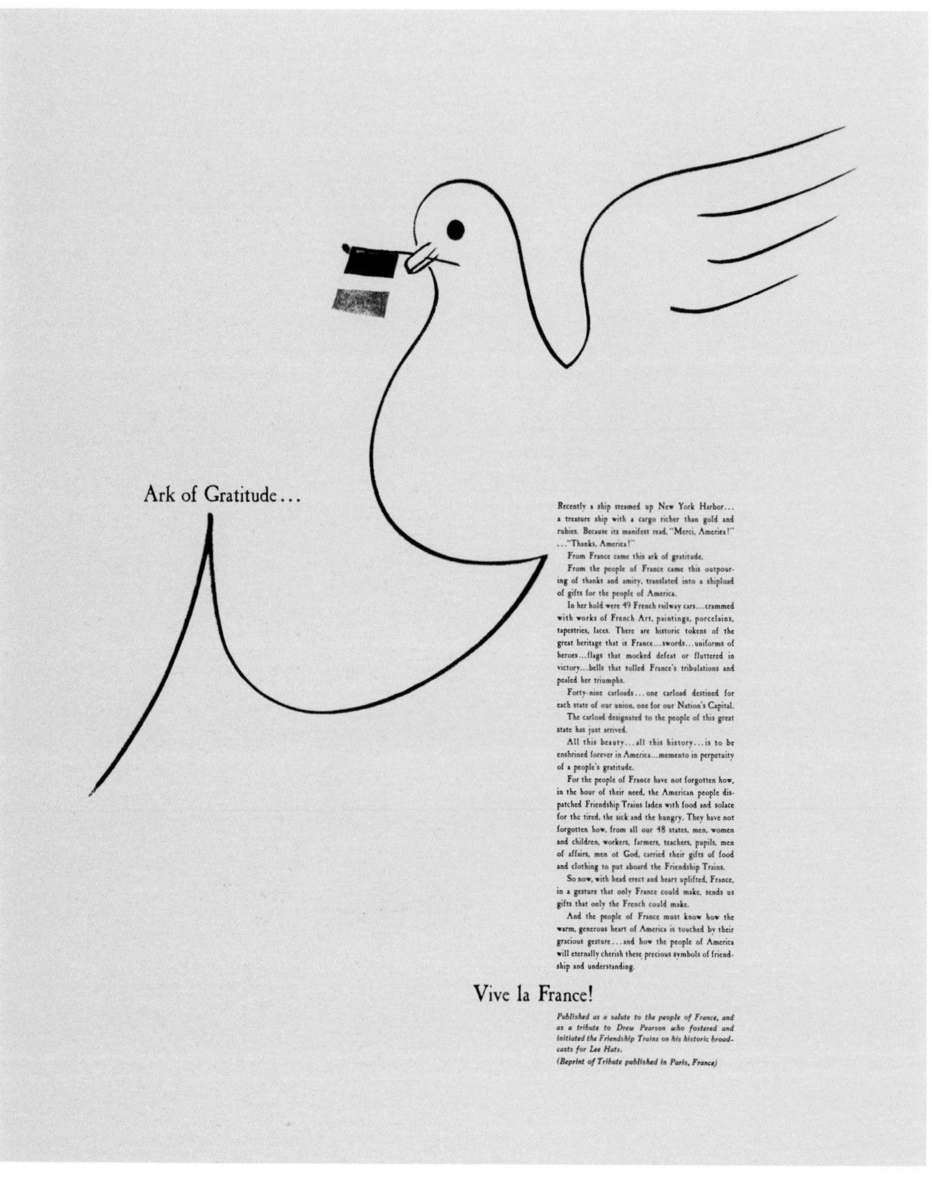

Ark of Gratitude...
Recently a ship steamed up New York Harbor... a treasure ship with a cargo richer than gold and rubies. Because its manifest read, "Merci, America!" ..."Thanks, America!"
From France came this ark of gratitude.
From the people of France came this outpouring of thanks and amity, translated into a shipload of gifts for the people of America.
In her hold were 49 French railway cars...crammed with works of French Art, paintings, porcelains, tapestries, laces. There are historic tokens of the great heritage that is France...swords...uniforms of heroes...flags that mocked defeat or fluttered in victory...bells that tolled France's tribulations and pealed her triumphs.
Forty-nine carloads...one carload destined for each state of our union, one for our Nation's Capital.
The carload designated to the people of this great state has just arrived.
All this beauty...all this history...is to be enshrined forever in America...memento in perpetuity of a people's gratitude.
For the people of France have not forgotten how, in the hour of their need, the American people dispatched Friendship Trains laden with food and solace for the tired, the sick and the hungry. They have not forgotten how, from all our 48 states, men, women and children, workers, farmers, teachers, pupils, men of affairs, men ot God, carried their gifts of food and clothing to put aboard the Friendship Trains.
So now, with head erect and heart uplifted, France, in a gesture that only France could make, sends us gifts that only the French could make.
And the people of France must know how the warm, generous heart of America is touched by their gracious gesture...and how the people of America will eternally cherish these precious symbols of friendship and understanding.
Vive la France!
Published as a salute to the people of France, and as a tribute to Drew Pearson who fostered and initiated the Friendship Trains on his historic broadcasts for Lee Hats.
(Reprint of Tribute published in Paris, France)

There are, however, instances when recognizable images are of sufficient plastic expressiveness to make the addition of geometric or abstract shapes superfluous.

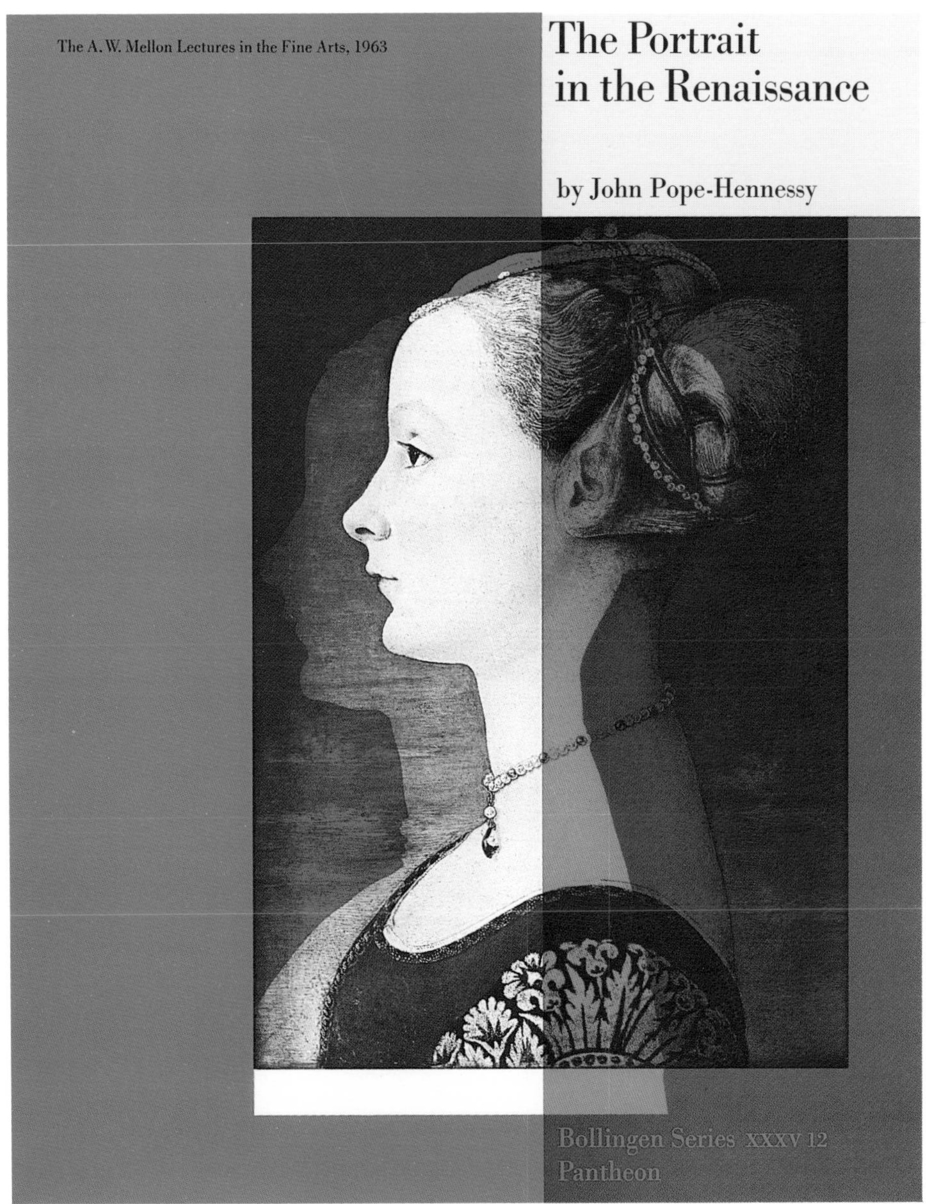

The A. W. Mellon Lectures in the Fine Arts, 1963
The Portrait
in the Renaissance
by John Pope-Hennessy
Bollingen Series XXXV 12
Pantheon

Magazine advertisement,
Westinghouse Electric Corporation,
1962

Jacket design,
Wittenborn, Schultz, Inc.,
1946

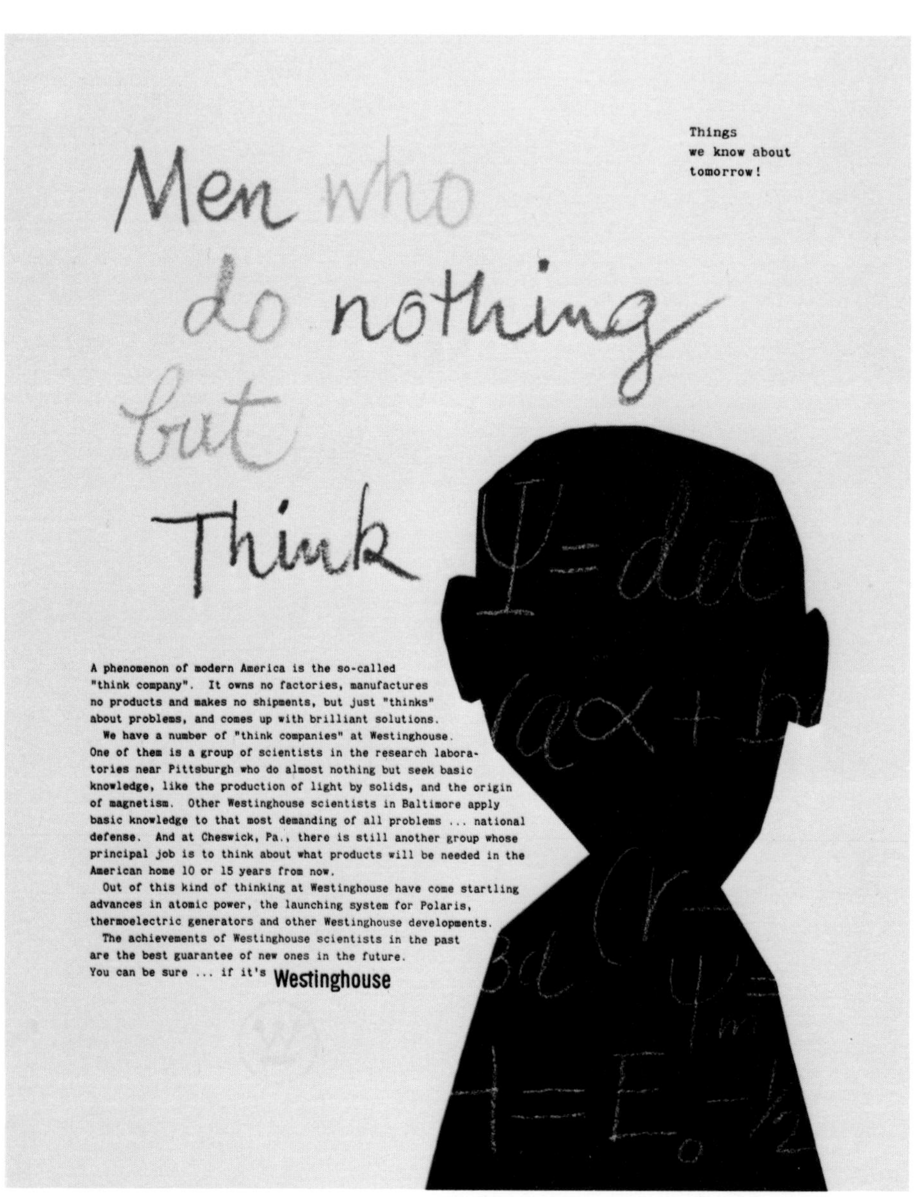

rigins of Modern Sculpture

Magazine advertisements,
Jacqueline Cochran,
1944

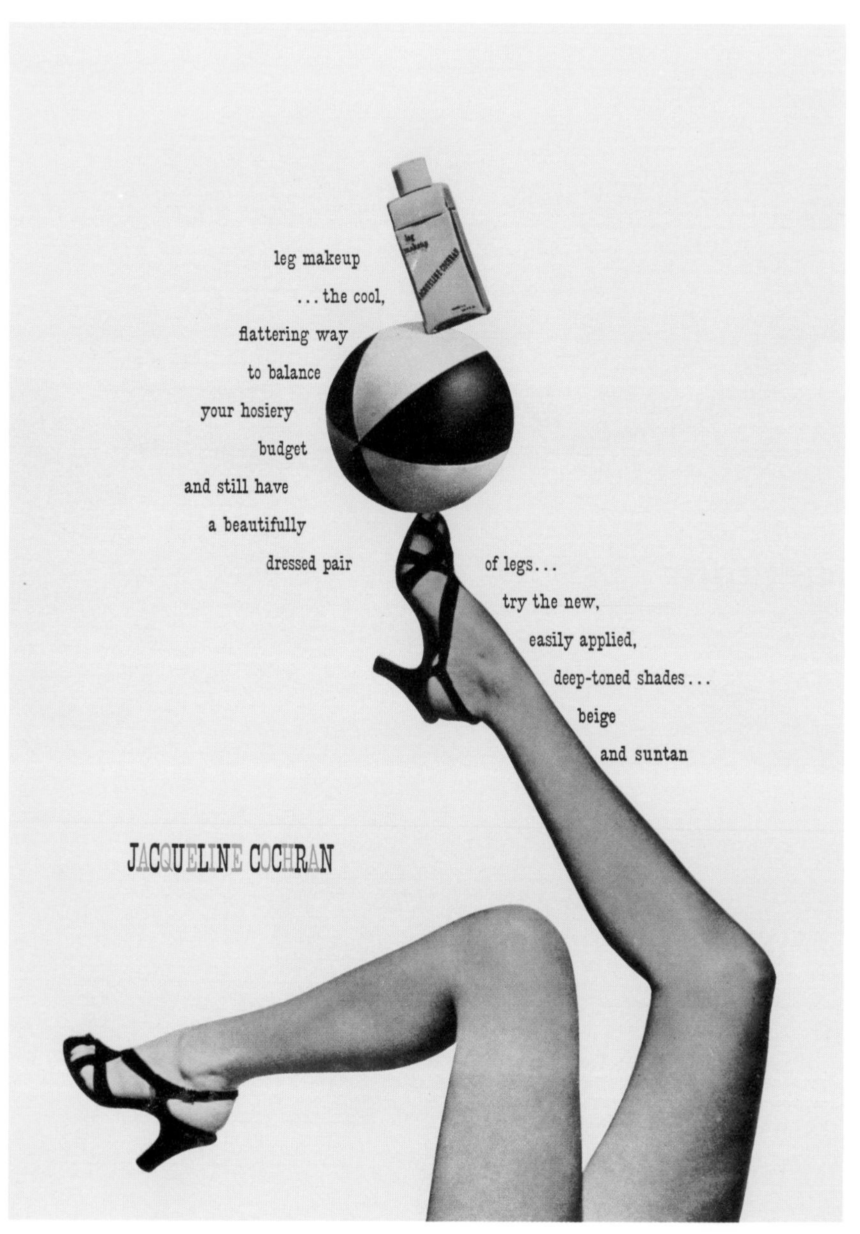

leg makeup
...the cool,
flattering way
to balance
your hosiery
budget
and still have
a beautifully
dressed pair
of legs...
try the new,
easily applied,
deep-toned shades...
beige
and suntan
JACQUELINE COCHRAN

1 merry-go-round twin . . . 2.00 plus tax
2 merry-go-round body lotion . . . 1.00 plus tax
3 merry-go-round puff . . . 1.25 plus tax

4 jacologne trio . . . 2.75 plus tax
5 jacologne flower garden . . . 9.75 plus tax
6 jacologne body sachet . . . 2.50 plus tax

7 pine bath bubbles . . . 2.00 and 1.00 plus tax
8 pine bath soap . . . 3 cakes boxed, 2.00

9 purse kit . . . 1.75 plus tax
10 sachet pillows . . . 2.50 plus tax
11 bath mitt . . . 2.00 plus tax

Jacqueline COCHRAN

Cover design,
Vintage,
1956

Jacket and book design,
Alfred A. Knopf,
1945

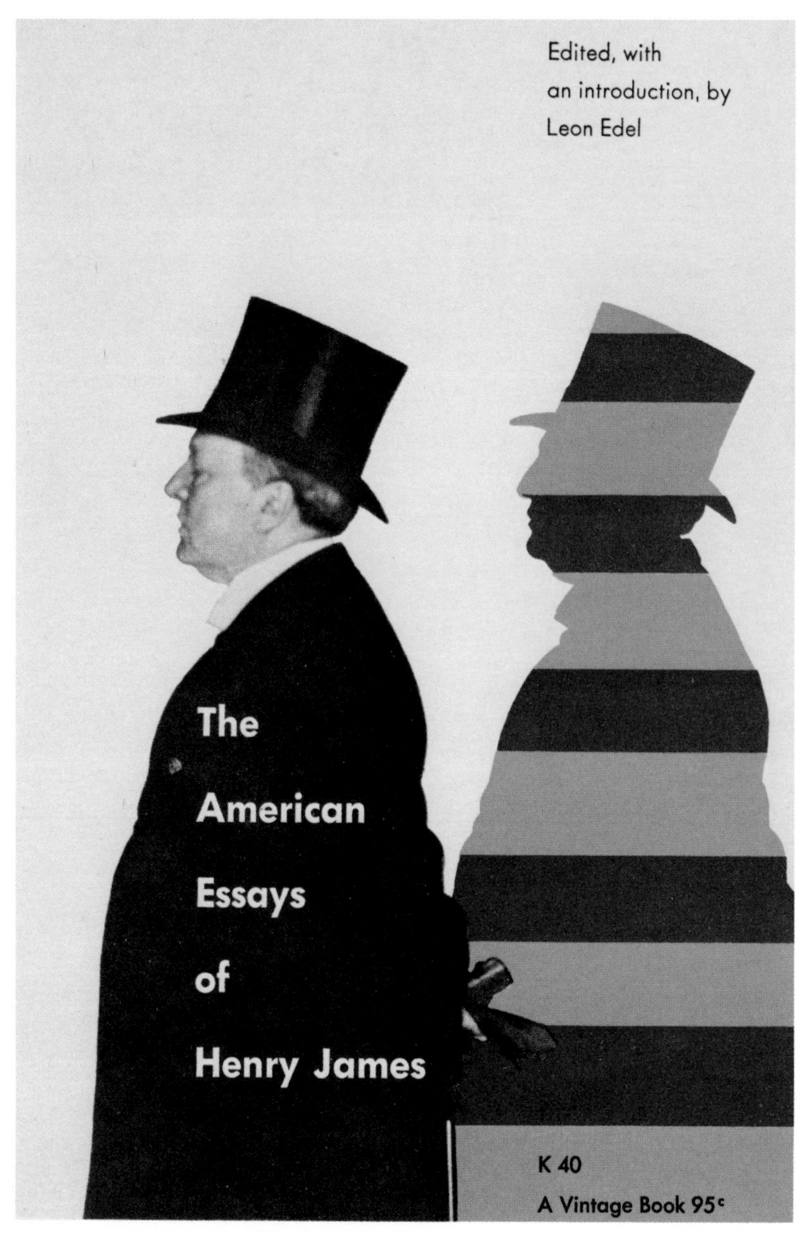

leave cancelled
monsarrat
leave
cancelled
by nicholas
monsarrat
leave cancelled
nicholas monsarrat
alfred a. knopf

Magazine cover,
Direction,
1943

Vol. 6. # 4

DIRECTION

25¢

Christmas 1943

Book illustration (variation),
Listen! Listen!
Harcourt Brace & World,
1970

Magazine advertisement,
Westinghouse Electric Corporation,
1963

To Catch a Hummingbird
How the Gemini Spacecraft will find its target . . .
Suppose you had to capture alive one little hummingbird flying a known course high over the Amazon jungle. Difficult? Sure, but no more so than the job assigned to a new radar system Westinghouse is building for the NASA-Gemini space program.
The bird is an Agena rocket, orbiting the earth at 17,500 miles per hour. The hunter, in an intersecting orbit, is the Gemini two-man spacecraft being built by McDonnell Aircraft. And so the hunt begins. The spacecraft radar finds the target and starts an electronic question-and-answer game. A computer keeps score, giving the astronauts continuous readings on angles and approach speeds until the vehicles are joined. The hummingbird is caught.
The Gemini experiments will be a prelude to the first moon trip. And Westinghouse is already working on advanced radar systems for lunar landings and deep space missions.
You can be sure . . . if it's Westinghouse.
We never forget how much you rely on Westinghouse.
Westinghouse

Magazine cover,
Direction,
1939

Jacket design,
Alfred A. Knopf,
1956

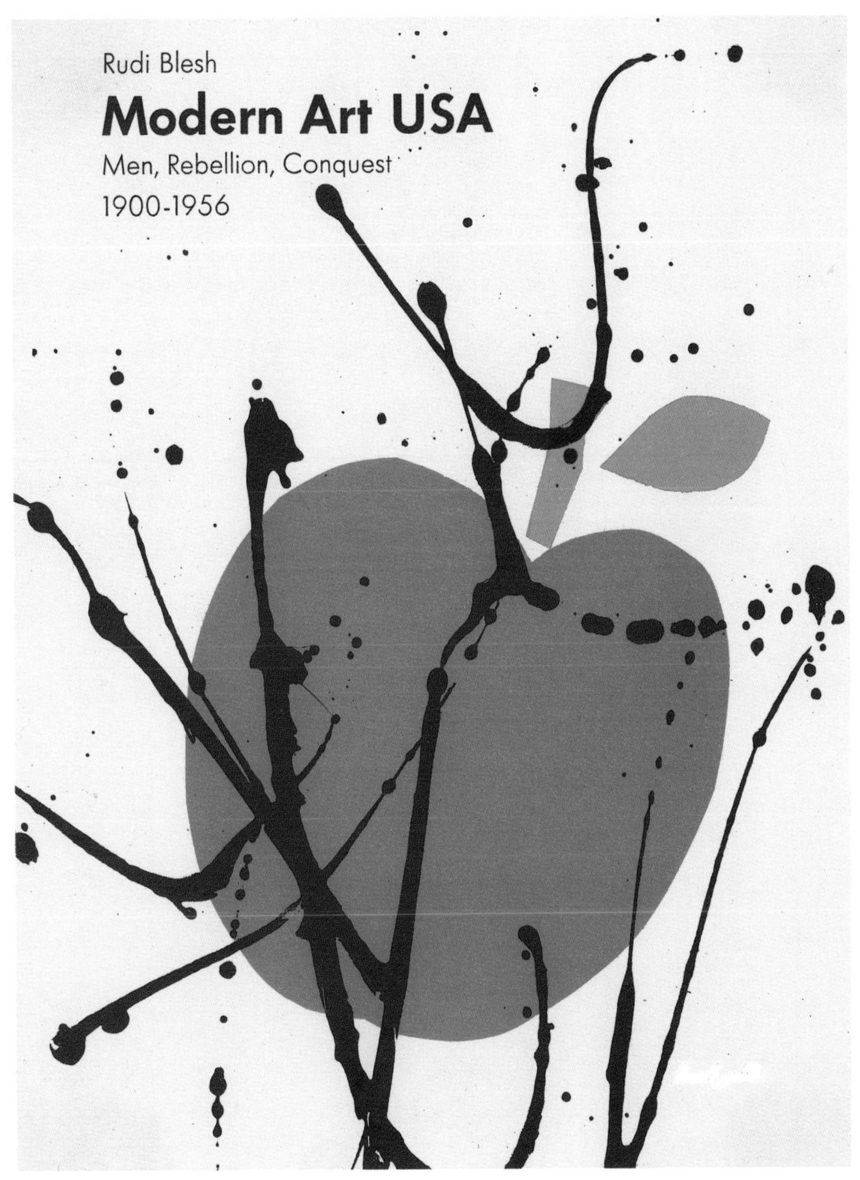
Rudi Blesh
Modern Art USA
Men, Rebellion, Conquest
1900-1956

Magazine cover,
Direction,
1941

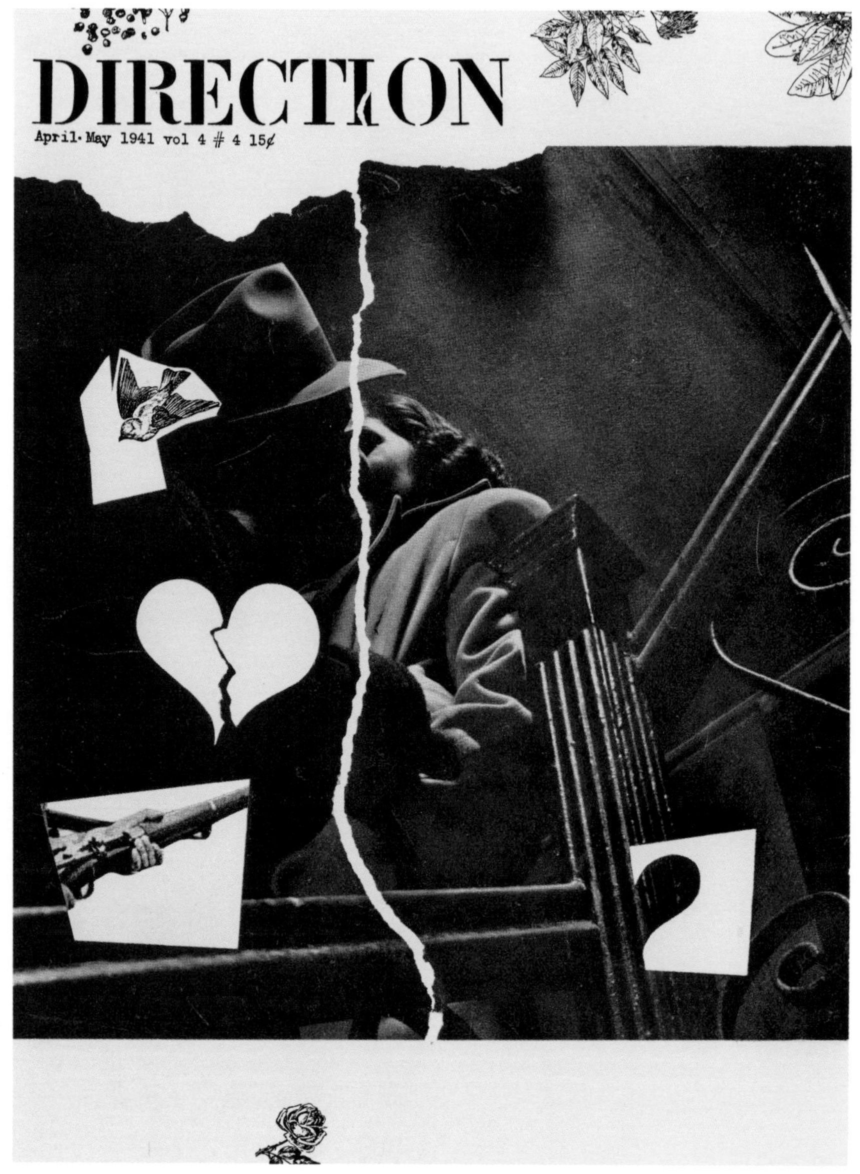

What we commonly understand as "originality" depends on the successful integration of the symbol as a visual entity with all other elements, pointed to a particular problem, performing a specific function consistent with its form. Its use at the proper time and place is essential and its misuse will inevitably result in banality or mere affectation. The designer's capacity to contribute to the effectiveness of the basic meaning of the symbol, by interpretation, addition, subtraction, juxtaposition, alteration, adjustment, association, intensification, and clarification, is parallel to those qualities that we call "original."

The Coronet Brandy advertisements are based on a common object – the brandy snifter – in animated form. The dot pattern of the soda bottle was designed to suggest effervescence; the dotted background is a visual extension of the bottle; the waiter is a variation of the snifter glass; the oval tray individualizes for Coronet the silver tray we used to see in liquor advertisements.

Etched goblet, Coronet Brandy, 1942

*Magazine advertisements,
Cresta Blanca Wine Company,
1946,
opposite, 1945,
overleaf, 1946*

CORONET
V.S.Q. BRANDY
delicious with soda
or ginger ale
VSQ
CORONET
VSQ
Fine Brandy
CORONET BRAN

VSQ
CORONET
VSQ
Fine Brandy
CORONET BRANDY

The dividing line between representational and nonrepresentational images is often very slim. In this advertisement for Ohrbach's the window shade acts as a formal as well as a poignantly suggestive image (1946).

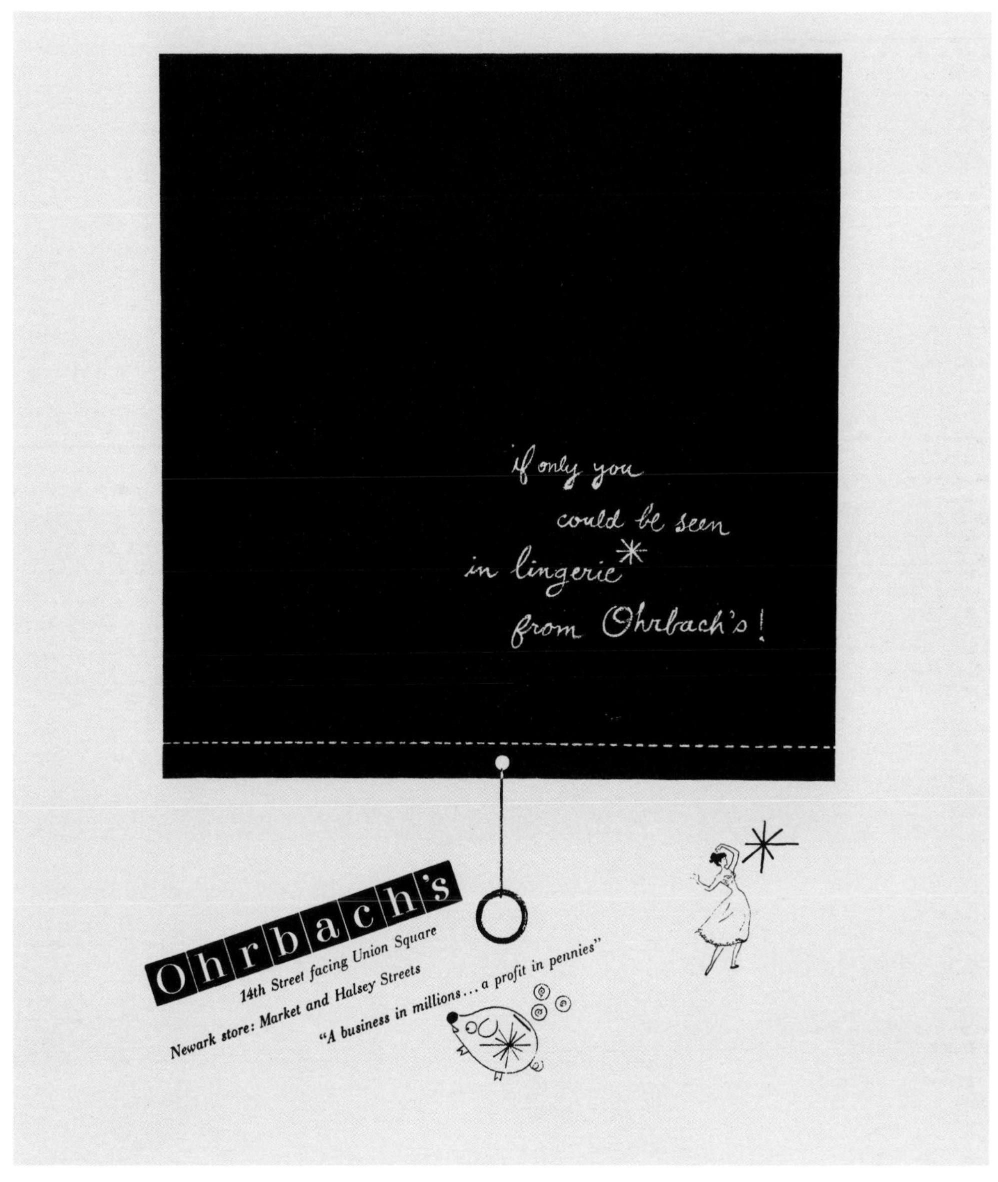

Occasionally purely nonrepresentational images function even more effectively without the support of explanatory illustrations – which tend to confine an idea and limit the imagination. The spectator is thus able to see more than is actually portrayed.

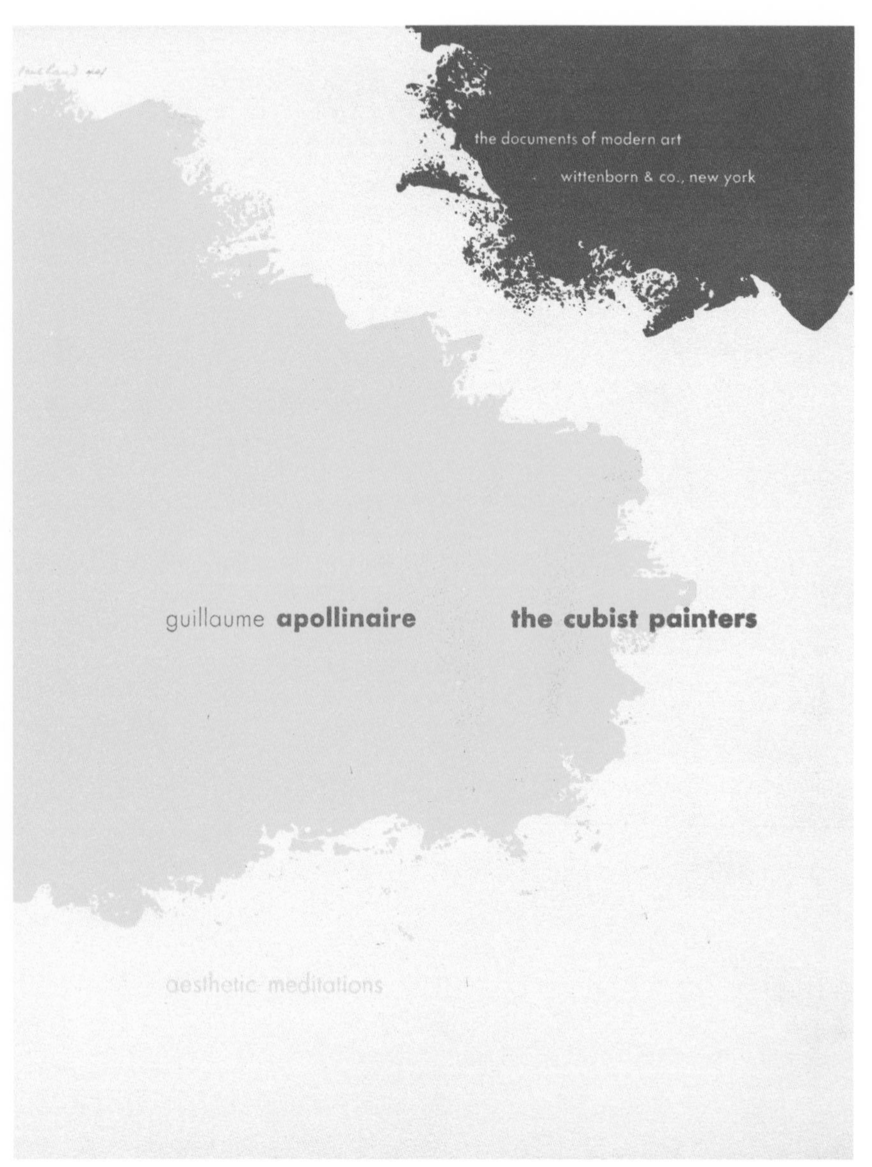

Jacket design, Pantheon, 1958

Cover design, Wittenborn & Company, 1944

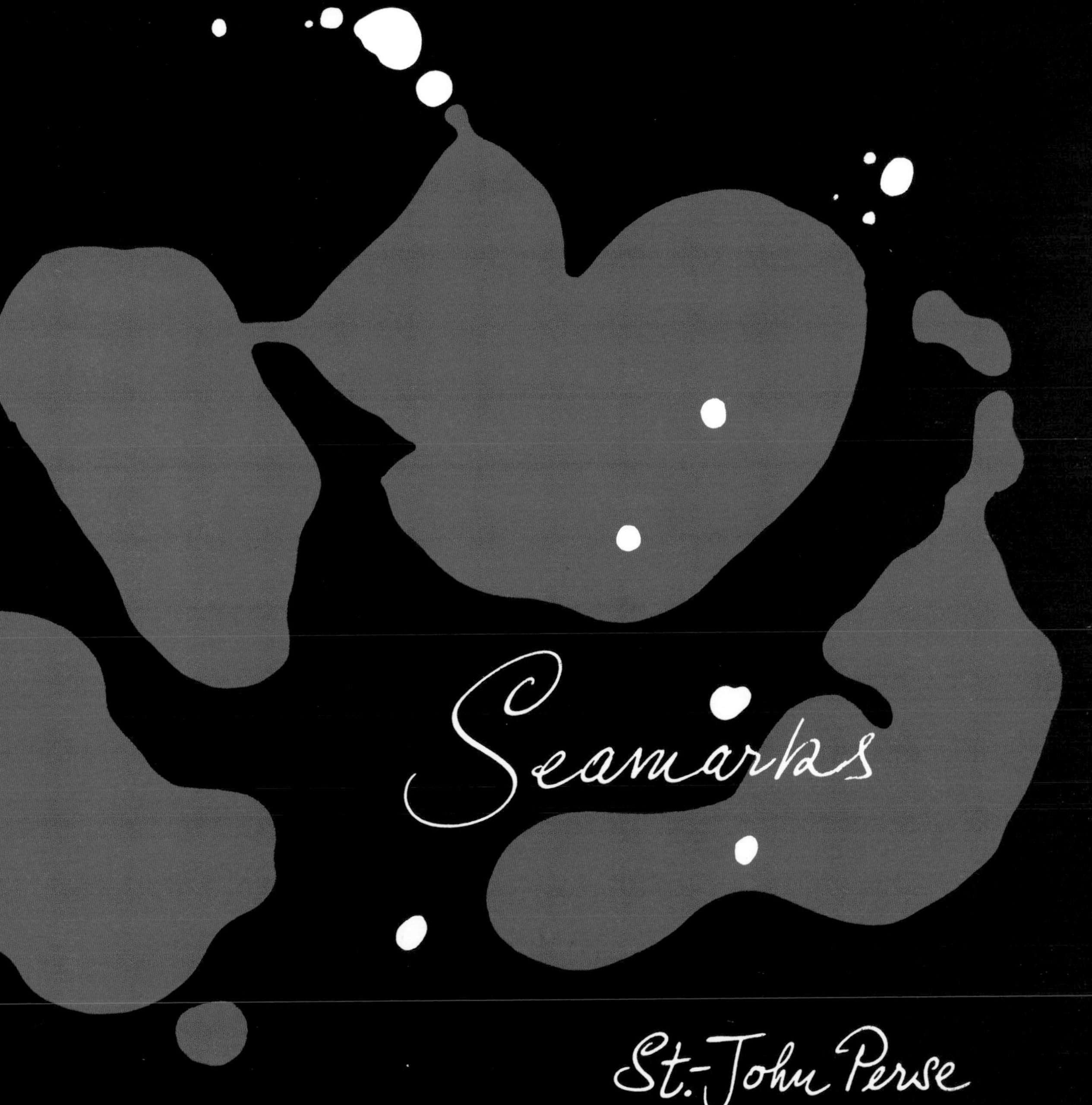

Translated by Wallace Fowlie

Bollingen Series LXVII

Pantheon

Jacket design,
Pantheon,
1962

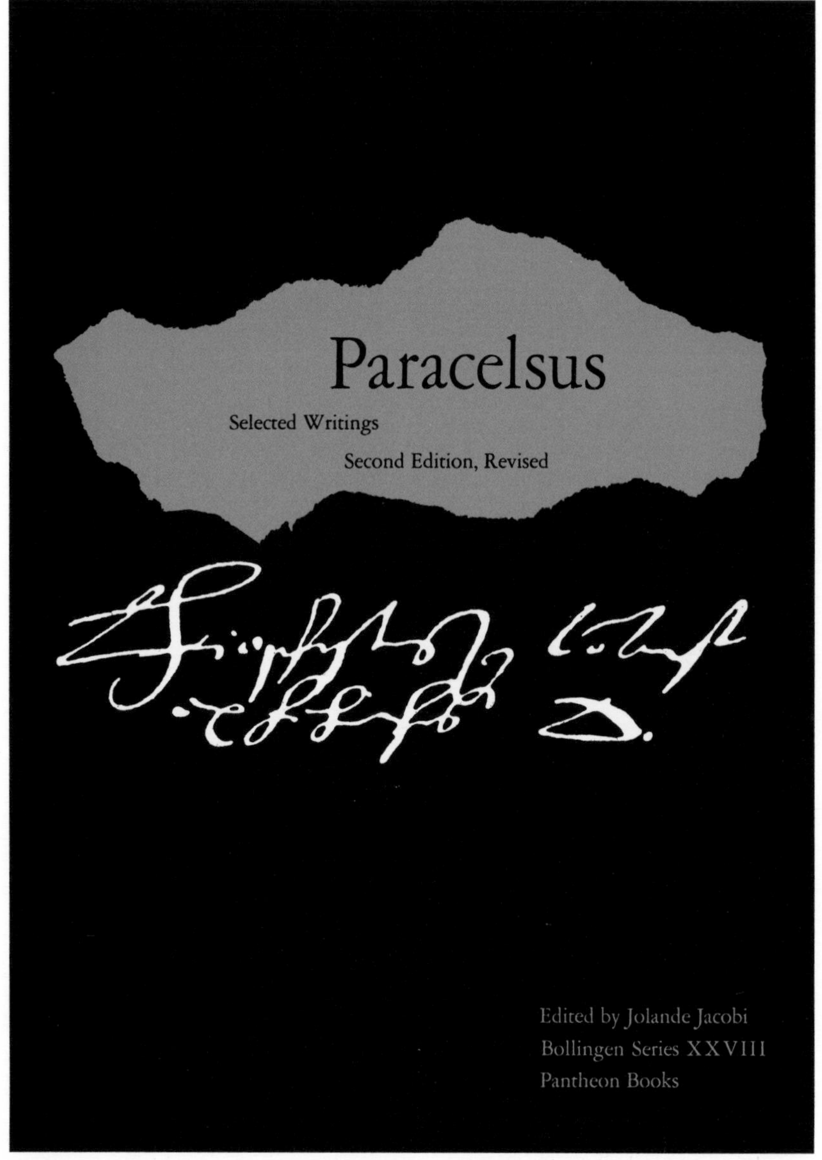

Paracelsus
Selected Writings
Second Edition, Revised
Edited by Jolande Jacobi
Bollingen Series XXVIII
Pantheon Books

Ideas About Ideas

The source of the creative impulse is a mystery. Where *do* ideas come from?

Any theory about inspiration must be offered with certain reservations. Ideas may come from anywhere, anything, any time, any place. For the most part, however, I believe that they spring from rather unromantic, sometimes unexpected, or even unsavory sources.

The artist is a collector of things imaginary or real. He accumulates things with the same enthusiasm that a little boy stuffs his pockets. The scrap heap and the museum are embraced with equal curiosity. He takes snapshots, makes notes, records impressions on tablecloths or newspapers, on backs of envelopes or matchbooks. Why one thing and not another is part of the mystery, but he is omnivorous.

Wildly heterogeneous as his inspirational treasures appear, curiosity is the common denominator and the pleasure of discovery an important by-product. The artist takes note of that which jolts him into visual awareness. Without the harvest of visual experience he would be unable to cope with the plethora of problems, mundane or otherwise, that confronts him in his daily work.

These stencils were purchased in a Paris paint shop many years ago. The possible applications were many and varied, from book jackets to fabrics to advertisements. Formal rather than historic or fashionable considerations were reasons for using this typeface.

Newspaper advertisement,
G.H.P. Cigar Company,
1957

Book jacket,
Alfred A. Knopf,
1956

You'll feel self-confident

with an **EL PRODUCTO**

MINE BOY

A novel by Peter Abrahams

Author of *Tell Freedom*

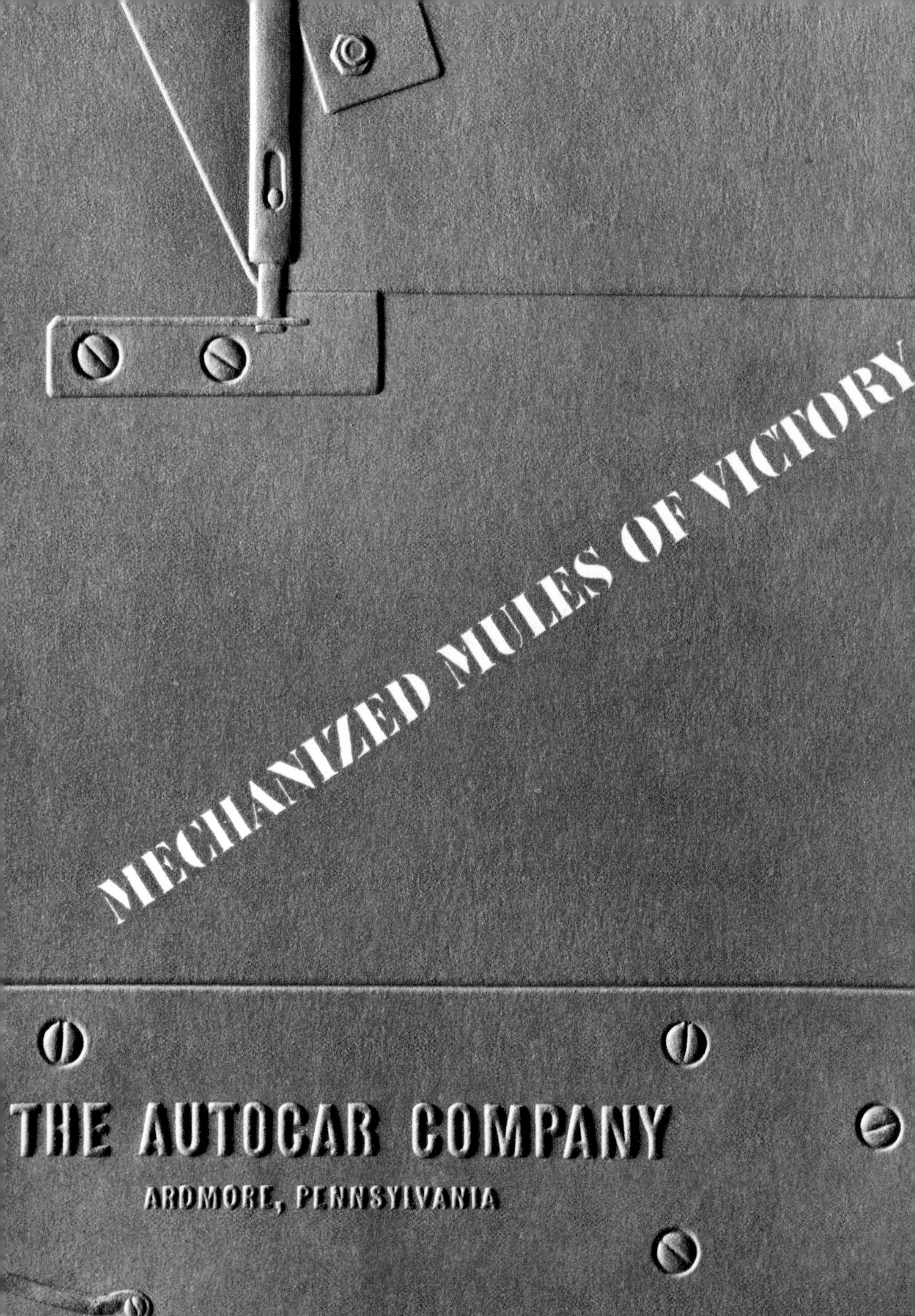
MECHANIZED MULES OF VICTORY
THE AUTOCAR COMPANY
ARDMORE, PENNSYLVANIA

rochure cover,
he Autocar Company,
942

Ideas may also grow out of the problem itself, which in turn becomes part of the solution. The coincidence of the letters OP in the magazine title with the initials of the company division name – Office Products – suggested this solution (IBM 1981).

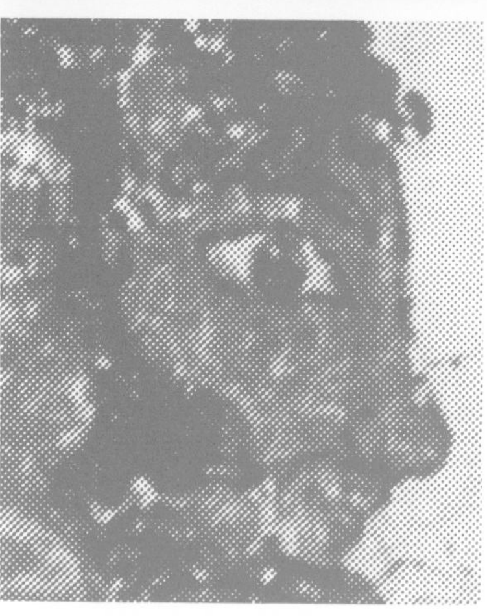

The sources of pictorial ideas are without limit: a visit to the museum, a casual glance at a picture postcard, or shop window, or something seen the day before in a book or newspaper are potential stores of inspiration. This profile with a staring eye, which I recalled seeing in a book on Etruscan art, prompted the idea for the illustration of this 1946 Container Corporation advertisement. The haunting eyes are germane to the message the advertisement is designed to convey.

THOMAS ERSKINE on the Advantages of Free Speech
When men can freely communicate their thoughts and their sufferings, real or imaginary, their passions spend themselves in air, like gunpowder scattered upon the surface; but pent up by terrors, they work unseen, burst forth in a moment, and destroy everything in their course.
(Rex v.Paine,1792)
Paul Rand

Great Ideas of Western Man...(one of a series) CONTAINER CORPORATION OF AMERICA

Announcement card, The American Advertising Guild, 1941

The American Advertising Guild
33 East 27 Street
announces an evening course in
Advertising Design
presenting a logical approach to the problems of layout in a series of laboratory sessions and forums directed by *Paul Rand.*

Aim: to create a new "graphic voice" by investigating: sources of inspiration . . . the relation of design to every day life . . . the logical use of elements and mediums . . . the organic application of forms to media.

10 sessions $25 . . . Guild members $15
Friday evenings from 7:30 to 9:30
beginning October 17, 1941.
Samples of work must be submitted when registering . . . Oct. 10 from 8 to 10 p.m.
Registration will be limited and accepted in order received.

The Meaning of Repetition

The emotional force generated by the repetition of words or pictures and the visual possibilities (as a means of creating texture, movement, rhythm, indicating equivalences of time and space) should not be minimized. The possibilities of repetition are limitless. Repeat patterns are only one familiar form. There is repetition of color, direction, weight, texture, dimension, movement, expression, shape, and so on. Repetition is an effective way of achieving unity.

The geometric patterns that adorn the surfaces of many Romanesque buildings demonstrate an awareness of the significance of unity, scale, and the decorative possibilities of repetition. The surprising and often humorous variations of the patterns are a lesson in how to avoid monotony.

Repetition also means remembrance. The efficacy of a trademark, for example, is dependent less on its design than on its repeated exposure to public view. Familiar things (e.g., dominoes on this page), as well as a touch of humor, are effective mnemonic devices.

The following are but a few instances of our everyday experiences in which the magical, almost hypnotic, effects of repetition operate: the exciting spectacle of marching soldiers in the same dress, same step, and same attitude; the fascination of neatly arranged flower beds of like color, structure, and texture; the impressive sight of crowds at football games, theatres, public demonstrations; the satisfaction we derive from the geometric patterns created by ballet dancers and chorus girls with identical costumes and movements; the feeling of order evoked by rows of methodically placed packages on the grocer's shelf; the comforting effect of the regularity of repeating patterns in textiles and wallpapers; the excitement we experience at the sight of plane formations or migrating flocks of birds.

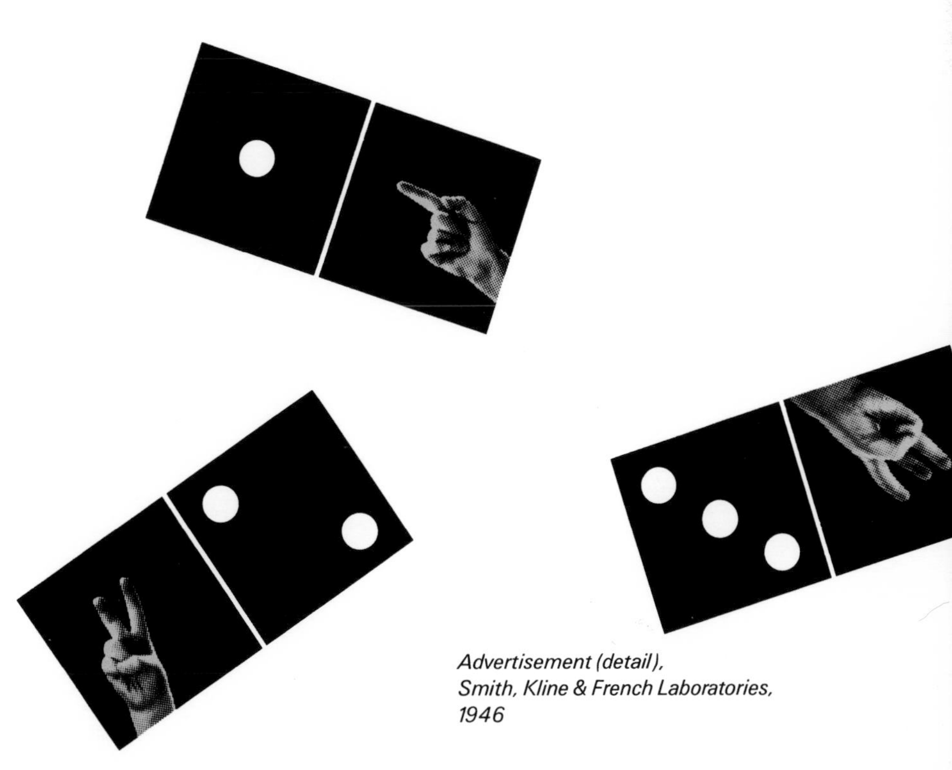

Advertisement (detail), Smith, Kline & French Laboratories, 1946

APPAREL ARTS

VOLUME

NUMBER

JULY–AUGUST, 19

$1.50 PER COP

Cover design, Apparel Arts, 1938

Advertisement, Dunhill Clothiers, 1947

DUNHILL

Letterhead,
Columbus, Indiana, Visitors Center,
1973

Folder,
IBM Corporation,
1984

506 Fifth Street
Columbus, Indiana
47201
812 372 1954

Paul Rand

IBM

Design
Program

Annual Report,
Irwin-Sweeney-Miller Foundation,
1971

Newspaper advertisement,
Frank H. Lee Co.,
1947

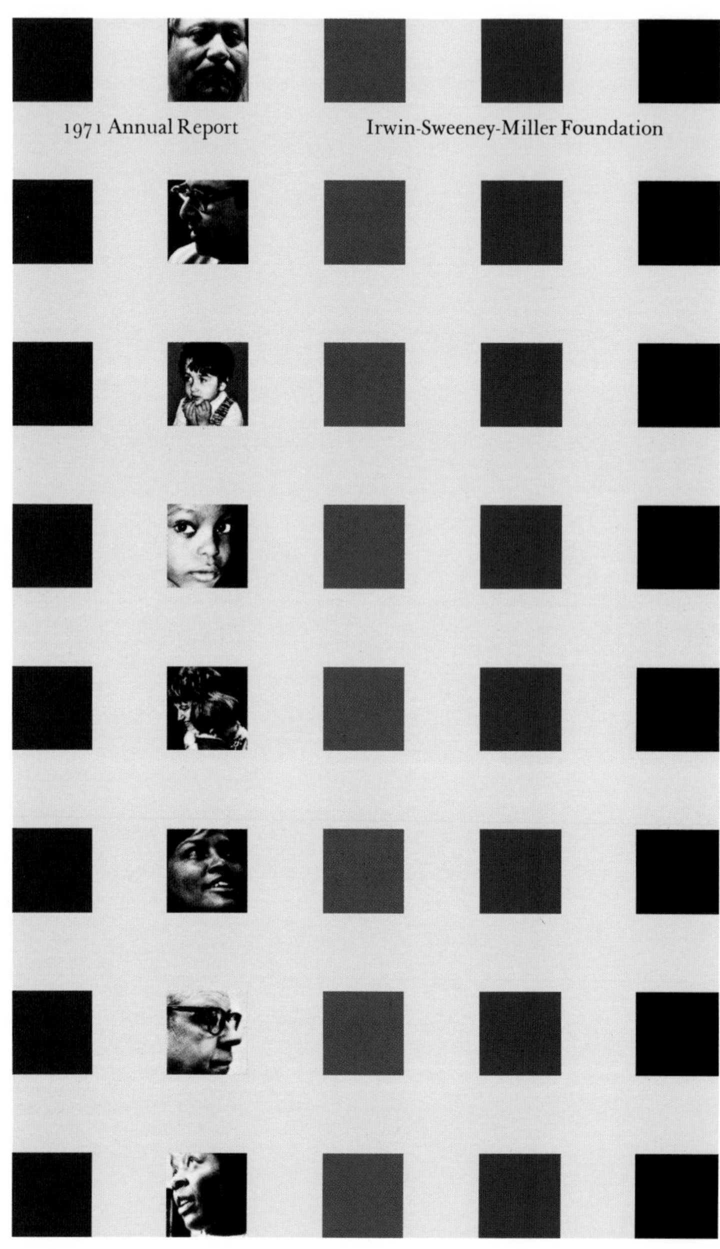

Bread Over The Waters

People of America: The food you piled on the Friendship Train has been delivered in Europe . . . a practical symbol of American good-will.

It said: Here is food for the hungry, hope for the hopeless, help that gives without question, that expects no reward.

But there is a reward. It is the still small voice of gratitude, the whisper that goes around the world blessing the name of America for help in a dark hour.

And over there, they praise the name of Drew Pearson, the man whose energetic compassion forged your instrument to turn aside the cruel blade of biting hunger . . . your Friendship Train.

To Drew Pearson, we say, well done! You are a faithful messenger of the American spirit.

It has been an honor and a privilege to have Drew Pearson initiate and foster the idea of your Friendship Train on his weekly broadcasts for Lee Hats.

Tune in Drew Pearson and his "Predictions of Things to Come" every Sunday, 6 p. m., coast-to-coast over the American Broadcasting Company network.

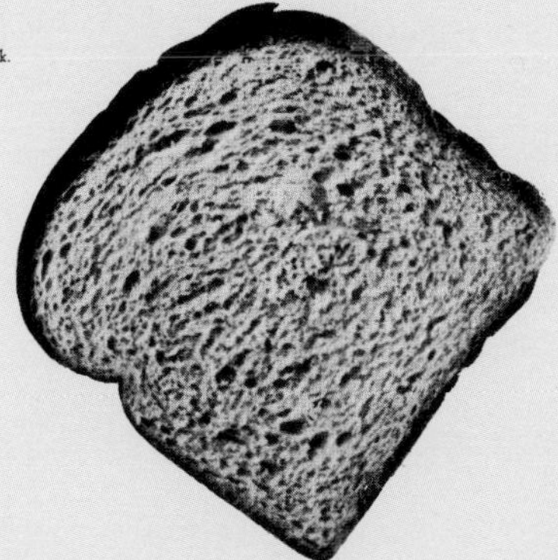

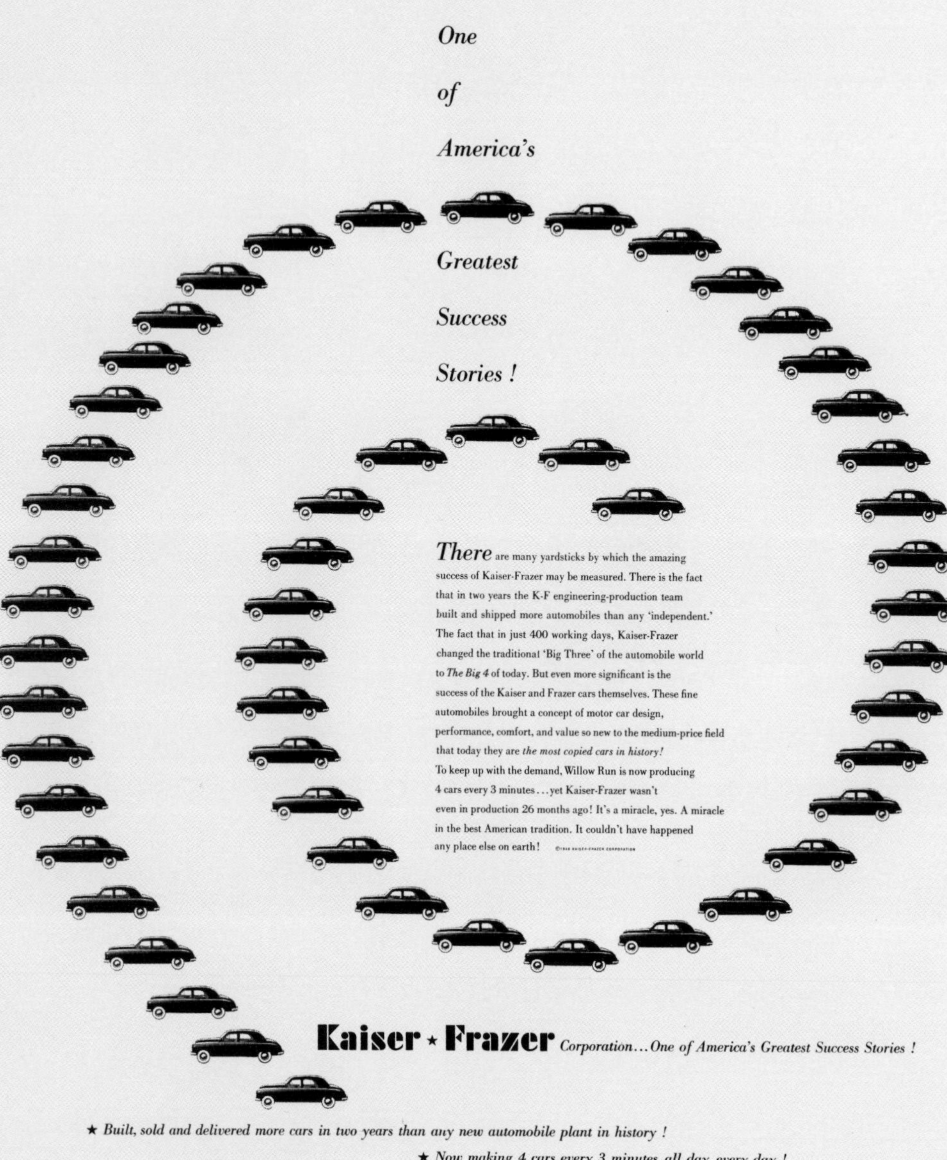

One
of
America's
Greatest
Success
Stories !
There are many yardsticks by which the amazing success of Kaiser-Frazer may be measured. There is the fact that in two years the K-F engineering-production team built and shipped more automobiles than any 'independent.' The fact that in just 400 working days, Kaiser-Frazer changed the traditional 'Big Three' of the automobile world to *The Big 4* of today. But even more significant is the success of the Kaiser and Frazer cars themselves. These fine automobiles brought a concept of motor car design, performance, comfort, and value so new to the medium-price field that today they are *the most copied cars in history!* To keep up with the demand, Willow Run is now producing 4 cars every 3 minutes . . . yet Kaiser-Frazer wasn't even in production 26 months ago! It's a miracle, yes. A miracle in the best American tradition. It couldn't have happened any place else on earth!
Kaiser ★ Frazer Corporation . . . One of America's Greatest Success Stories !

★ Built, sold and delivered more cars in two years than any new automobile plant in history !

★ Now making 4 cars every 3 minutes, all day, every day !

★ Originators of the most copied cars in history !

★ Largest "independent" . . . now the old 'Big Three' is The Big 4 !

★ One of the largest Dealer-Service organizations in the world !

Advertisement,
Kaiser-Frazer Corporation,
1948

Illustration,
Stafford Fabrics,
1944

Magazine cover,
Direction,
1943

Poster,
Museum of Modern Art,
1949

The House in the Museum Garden

Marcel Breuer, Architect

Museum of Modern Art, New York

Entrance: 4 West 54 Street

Admission: 35 cents Daily 12 to 7, Sunday 1 to 7

Cover design,
IBM Corporation,
1982

Magazine cover,
Idea: International Advertising Art,
1955

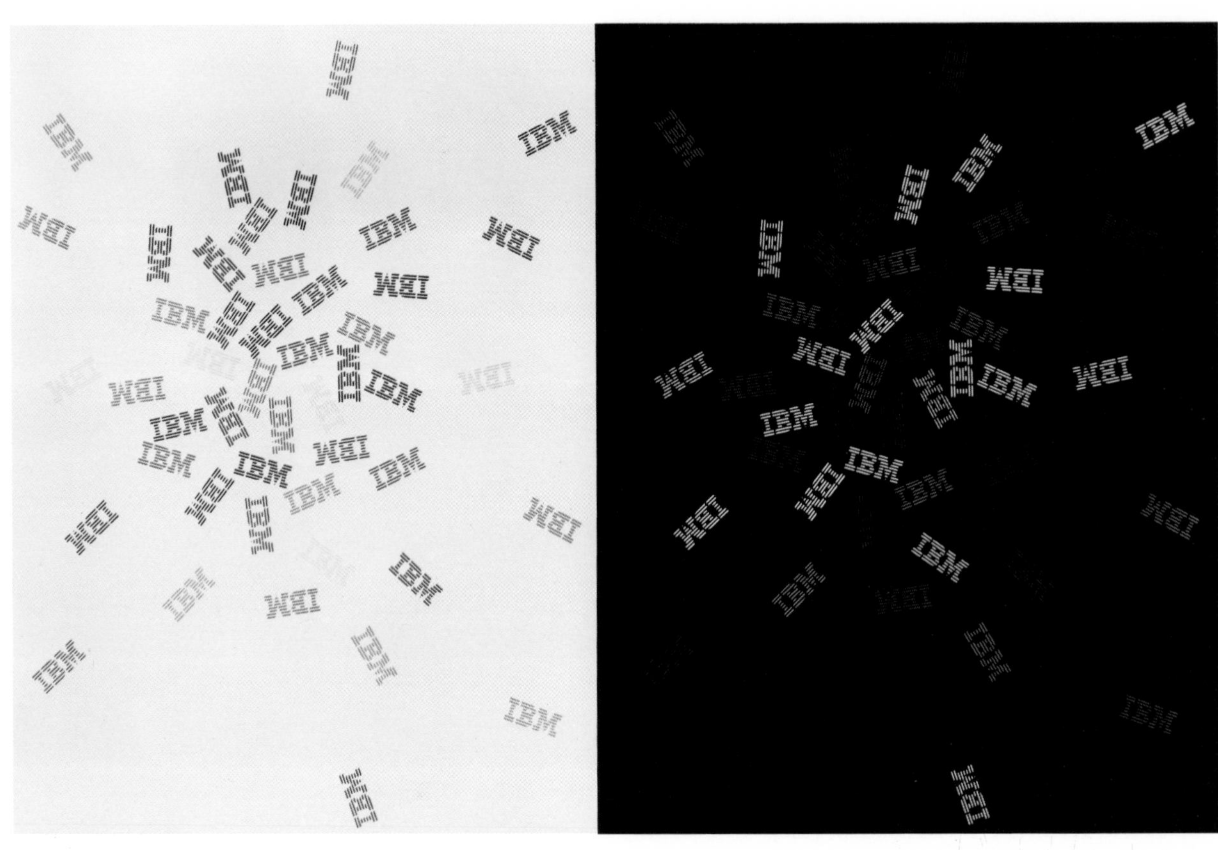

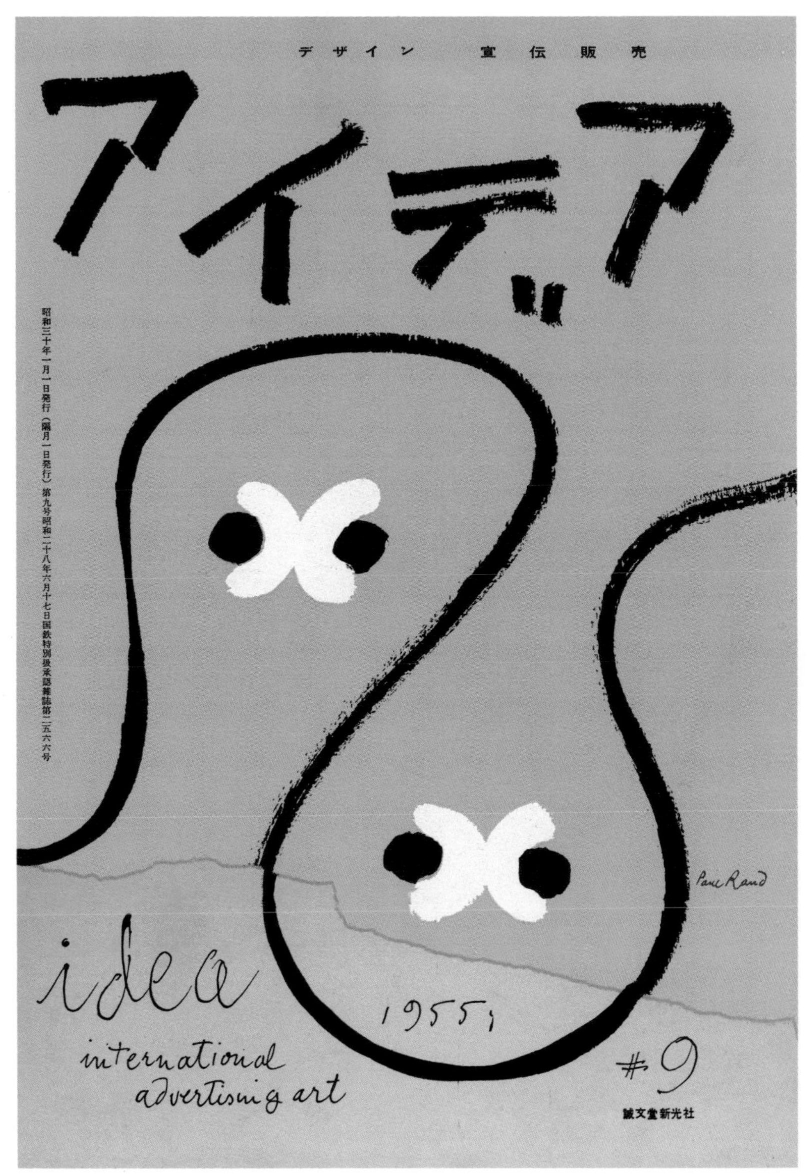
デザイン　宣伝販売
アイデア
昭和三十年一月一日発行（隔月一日発行）第九号昭和二十八年六月十七日国鉄特別扱承認雑誌第二五六六号
Paul Rand
idea
1955
international advertising art
#9
誠文堂新光社

The Role of Humor

Readership surveys demonstrate the significance of humor in the field of visual communication. The reference is not principally to cartoon strip advertisements or to out-and-out gags, but to a more subtle variety, one indigenous to the design itself and achieved by means of association, juxtaposition, size relationship, proportion, space, or special handling.

The visual message that professes to be profound or elegant often boomerangs as mere pretension; and the frame of mind that looks at humor as trivial and flighty mistakes the shadow for the substance. In short, the notion that the humorous approach to visual communication is undignified or belittling is sheer nonsense. This misconception has been discredited by those entrepreneurs who have successfully exploited humor as a means of creating confidence, goodwill, and a receptive frame of mind toward an idea or product. Radio and television commercials have made tremendous strides in the use of humor as a potent sales device. And, as an aid to understanding serious problems in war training, as an effective weapon in safety posters,[1] war bond selling, and morale building, humor was neglected by neither government nor civilian agencies in time of war.

Stressing the profound effects of entertainment, Plato, in *The Republic,* declares: "Therefore do not use compulsion, but let early education be rather a sort of amusement." The arts of ancient China,[2] India, and Persia reflect a humorous spirit in the design of masks, ceramics, and paintings. American advertising in its infancy also demonstrated this tendency toward humor in, for example, the cigar store Indian and the medicine man. That humor is a product of serious contemporary thought is revealed in the significant paintings and sculptures by, for instance, Picasso, Miro, Ernst, Duchamp, Dubuffet. "True humor," says Thomas Carlyle, "springs not more from the head than from the heart; it is not contempt, its essence is love, it issues not in laughter, but in still smiles, which lie far deeper."

1 *Printers' Ink,* December 28, 1946.

2 Roger Fry, "Some Aspects of Chinese Art," *Transformations,* 79–81.

Trade advertisement,
Smith, Kline & French Laboratories,
1945

Cover design,
American Institute of Graphic Art,
1968

With children... "...the benzedrine inhaler can be satisfactorily employed for young children for the relief of obstructive symptoms in the nasopharynx due either to infection or to allergic edema. No untoward symptoms were noted from the use of the inhaler." Vollmer, E.S.: Use of the Benzedrine Inhaler for Children, Arch. Otolaryng., 26:91.

Benzedrine Inhaler a better means of nasal medication

In a recent survey of pediatricians, 77% were found to use Benzedrine Inhaler, N.N.R., in their practice.
The ease of application which makes Benzedrine Inhaler so useful with adults is even more important in treating the congestion occurring in children's head colds.
Children accept Benzedrine Inhaler therapy willingly, and show none of the hostility which so often complicates the administration of drops, tampons, or sprays. Each Benzedrine Inhaler is packed with racemic amphetamine, S.K.F., 200 mg.; menthol, 10 mg.; and aromatics. Smith, Kline & French Laboratories, Philadelphia, Pa.

Paul Rand

Poster,
G.H.P. Cigar Company,
1958

Book illustration,
Listen! Listen!
Harcourt Brace & World,
1970

Christmas rolls 'round again ... with its merry voices, smiling faces, happy meetings. It is a time to be gay, but also a time to review all the things we hope and wish for.

Above all else, we hope and wish for peace and tranquility at home and among the nations.

Above all else, we are grateful for the manifold blessings that flow from the good fortune of living in this wonderful land of ours.

Also, we of G.H.P. are sincerely grateful for the many warm associations we have made and maintained in our world of business. Each passing year makes it more pleasant to pass this appreciation on to you.

And so please accept our sincere wishes for a happy holiday season for you and your family. May the coming year bring you all good things - health and happiness, peace and prosperity.

December, 1952 G.H.P. Cigar Company, Inc.

Poster,
G.H.P. Cigar Company,
1952

Advertisement,
Kaiser-Frazer Corporation,
1948

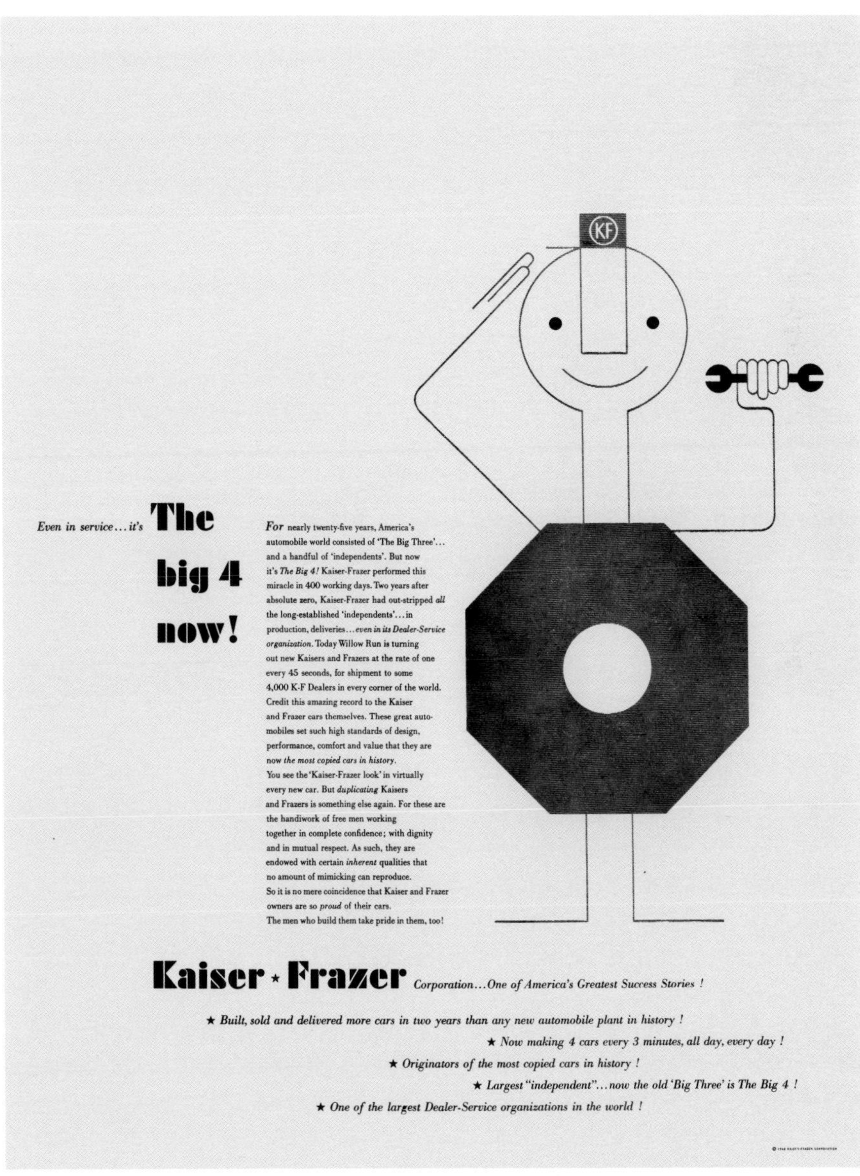

Advertisers of pharmaceuticals, more circumspect than others, use the light touch of humor for its soothing and profitable results.

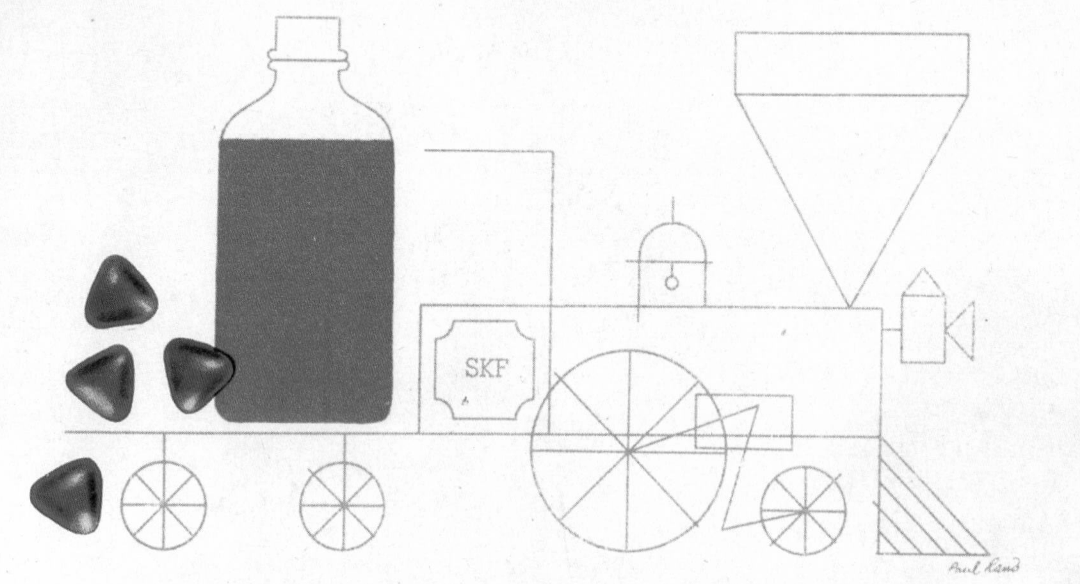
From the Menarche to the Menopause . . .Woman requires 4 times as much iron as man.
SKF
Paul Rand

Prospectus,
Smith, Kline & French Laboratories,
1946

Poster,
Interfaith Day Movement, Inc.,
1954

Interfaith Day

Sunday September 26, 1 p.m.

Central Park Mall

All Star Program

Jacket design,
Rinehart and Company,
1946

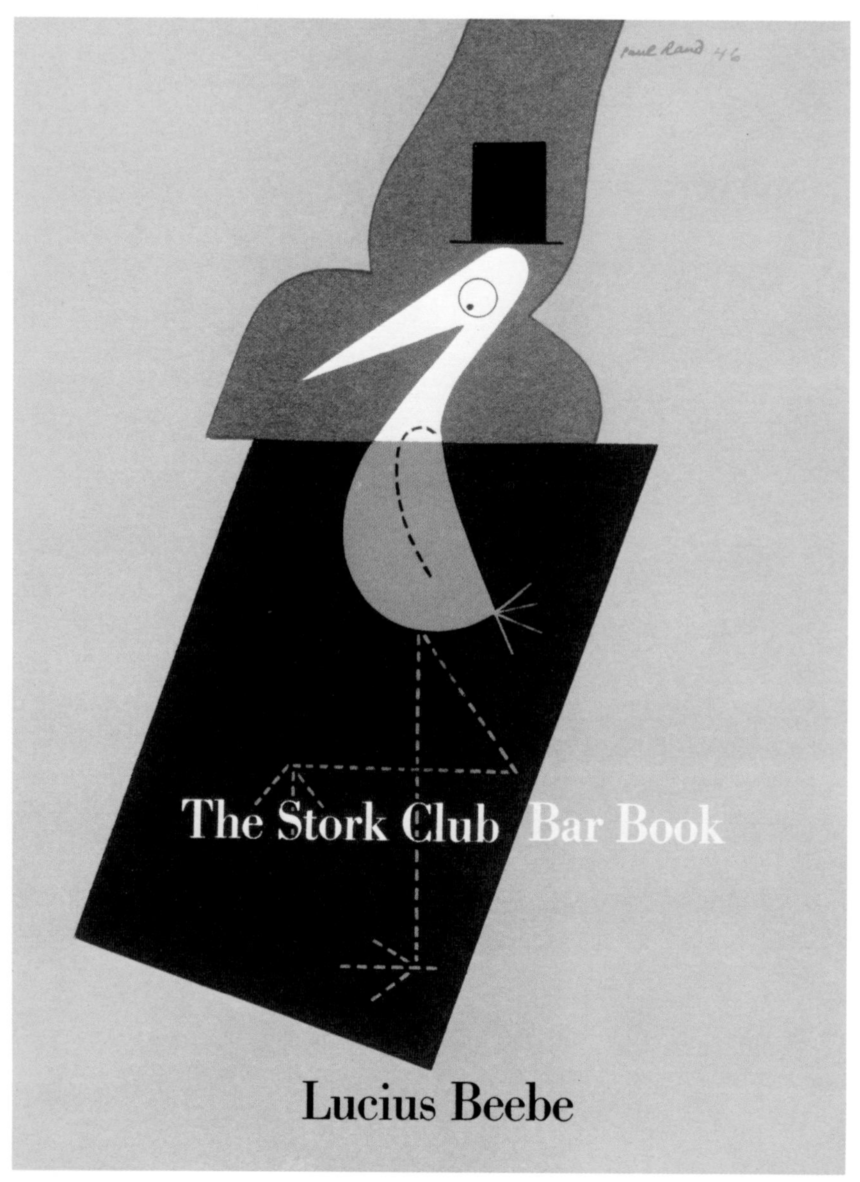

The kind of humor expressed by the "Dubonnet man" (originated by Cassandre) is inherent in the design itself. The funny face and general attitude seem to suggest rather than to illustrate *a quality of conviviality. To adapt this figure for an American audience, the problem was to impart this same spirit without altering the original visual conception.*

Magazine advertisement (detail),
Dubonnet Corporation,
1942

Magazine advertisements,
Dubonnet Corporation,
1943

DUBONNET
Dubonnet
wine
An Aperitif
MADE SINCE 1846
MADE AND BOTTLED IN U.S.A.
BY DUBONNET CORPORATION
PREPARED BY AUTHORITY OF
Sweet
VERMOUTH
Dubonnet

The Rebus and the Visual Pun

A single letter says more than a thousand words. The dual reading is what makes such images memorable. They amuse as they inform. The U symbol is an experiment in visual puns, as is the cover design for AIGA, which combines a rebus (the eye for the letter I) and a collection of letters to produce a mask. Of the twenty-six letters of the alphabet, the letters B and I are clearly the most graphic and least subject to misinterpretation. The rebus is a mnemonic device, a kind of game designed to engage the reader and, incidentally, lots of fun.

The development of any visual image must begin with some tangible idea, conscious or otherwise. It should come as no surprise that, more often than not, creative ideas are the product of chance, intuition, or accident, later justified to fit some prevailing popular theory, practical need, or formal obsession.

*Cover design,
AIGA, 50 Books,
1972*

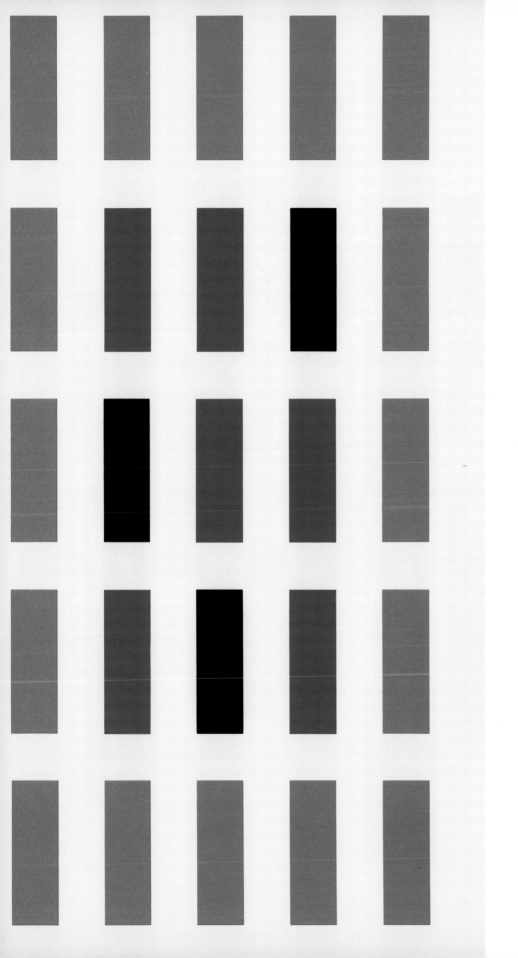

Letters of the alphabet turn into piano keys. The name of Chopin reinforces the pun.

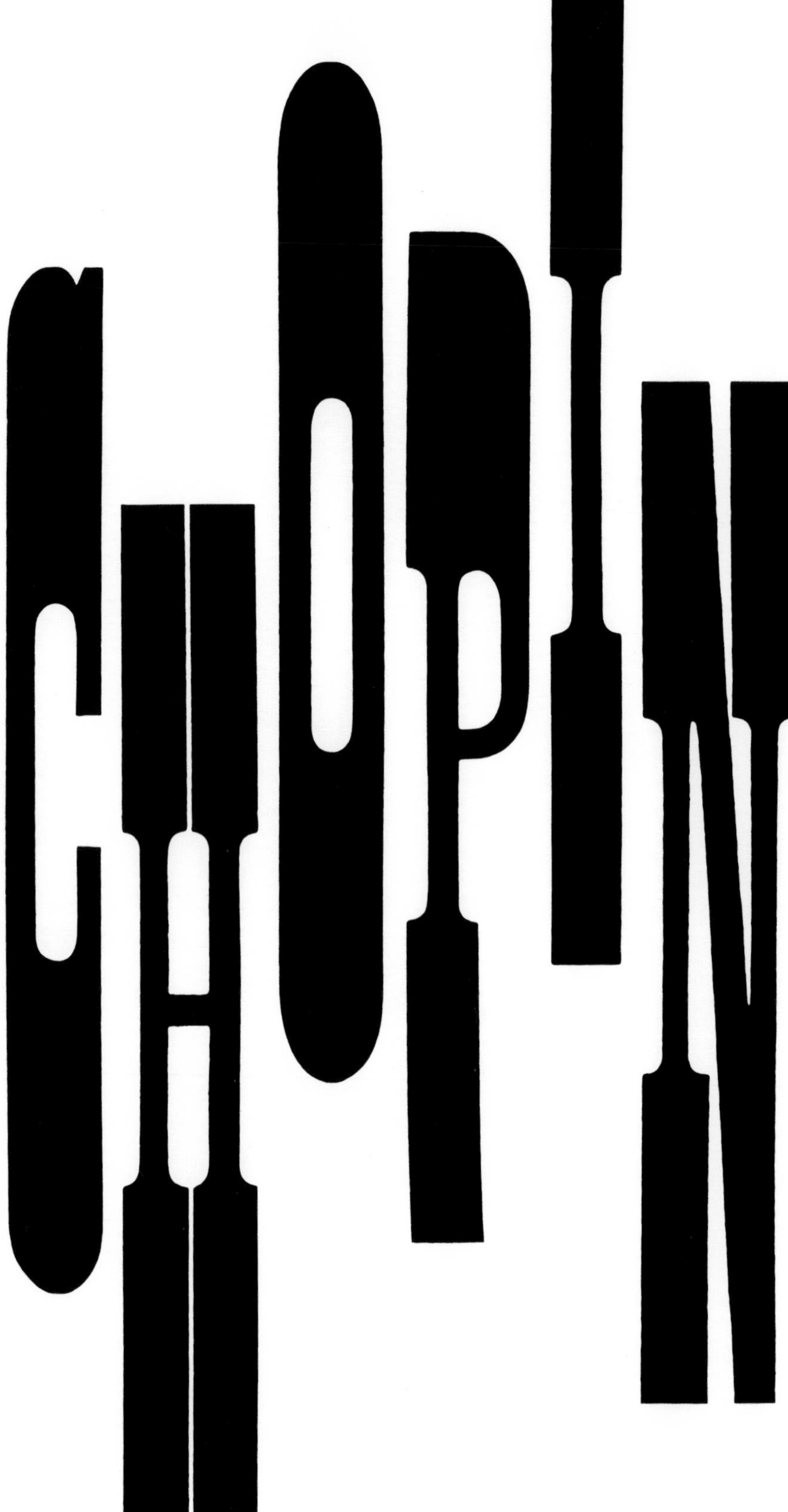

Advertisement,
Westinghouse Electric Corporation,
1971

Prospectus,
New York Art Directors Club,
1983

The visual pun, in which a double meaning is projected graphically, may assume many different forms. The dots in this illustration read as eyes or buttons or flowers or bees or olives or snakes or fish, etc., depending on the context.

Jacket design,
Alfred A. Knopf, Zokeisha
1959

Newspaper advertisement,
Ohrbach's,
1946

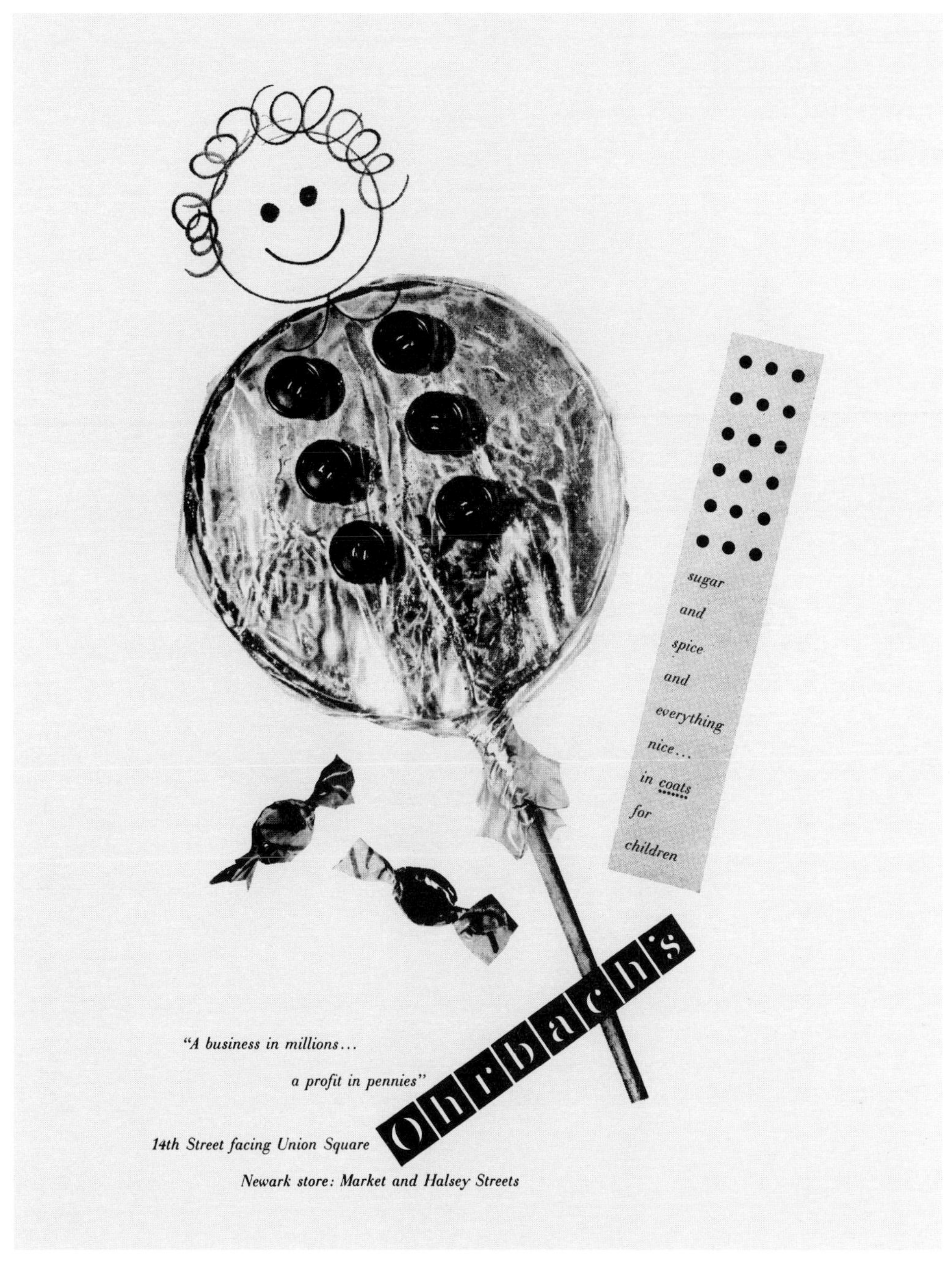

Cover design,
Alfred A. Knopf,
1960

Book illustration,
I Know a Lot of Things,
Harcourt Brace & World,
1956

Oh
I know
such
a
lot
of
things,
but
as
I
grow
I know
I'll
know
much
more.

Cover design,
Harvest Books,
1955

Book cover illustration,
Alfred A. Knopf,
1956

Visual interpretation of Maurice Denis's 1890 definition of Neotraditionism, (Design Quarterly, 1984).

"It is well to remember

that a Picture — before

a , or some

is essentially a plane

covered with

in a certain order"

being a  ,

Anecdote—

surface

assembled

Jacket design,
Alfred A. Knopf,
1955

Cover design,
Museum of Modern Art,
1949

The Museum of Modern Art
Modern Art in Your Life

A printed circuit and simple silhouette of a hand suggest both player and instrument.

Prospectus,
Yale University School of Art,
1982

Exposicion
de pintura
contemporanea
norteamericana.

Poster,
Museum of Modern Art,
1941

Poster,
U.S. Department of the Interior,
1975

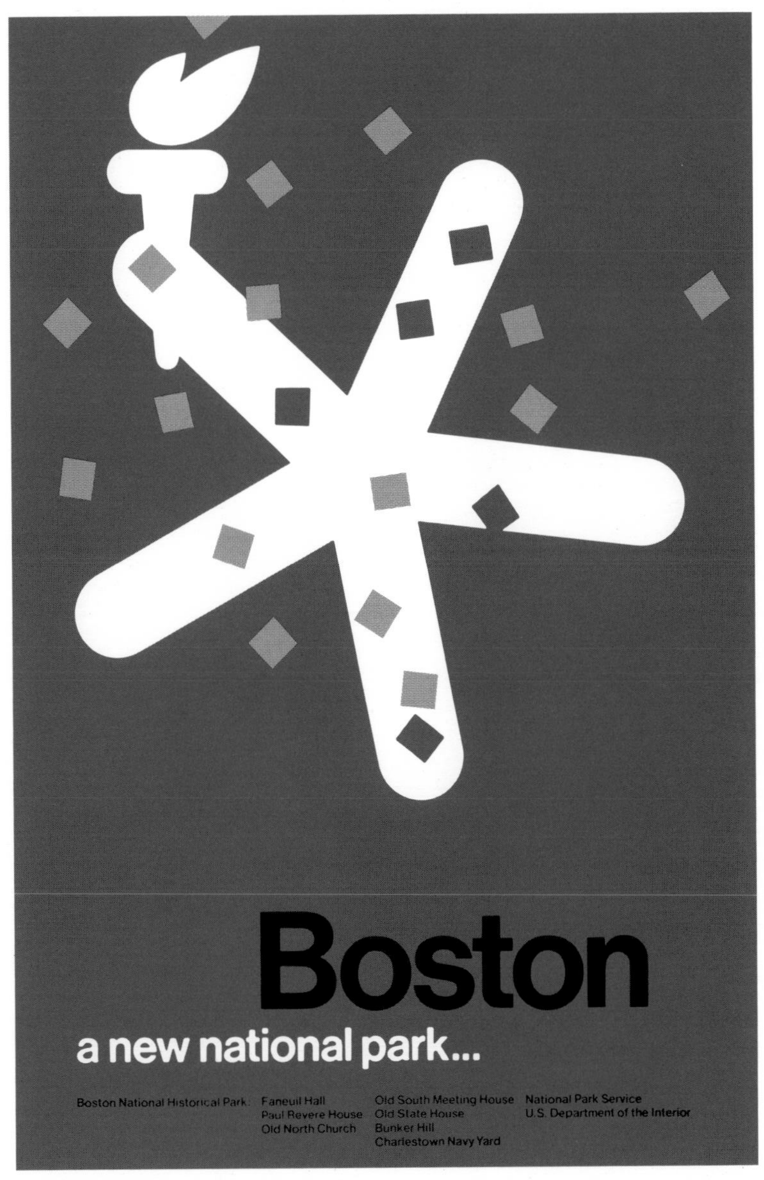

The "visual pun" can be as persuasive as it is informative and entertaining.

Advertisement,
G.H.P. Cigar Company,
1952

Poster,
IBM Corporation,
1981

Magazine cover,
Jazzways Inc.,
1946

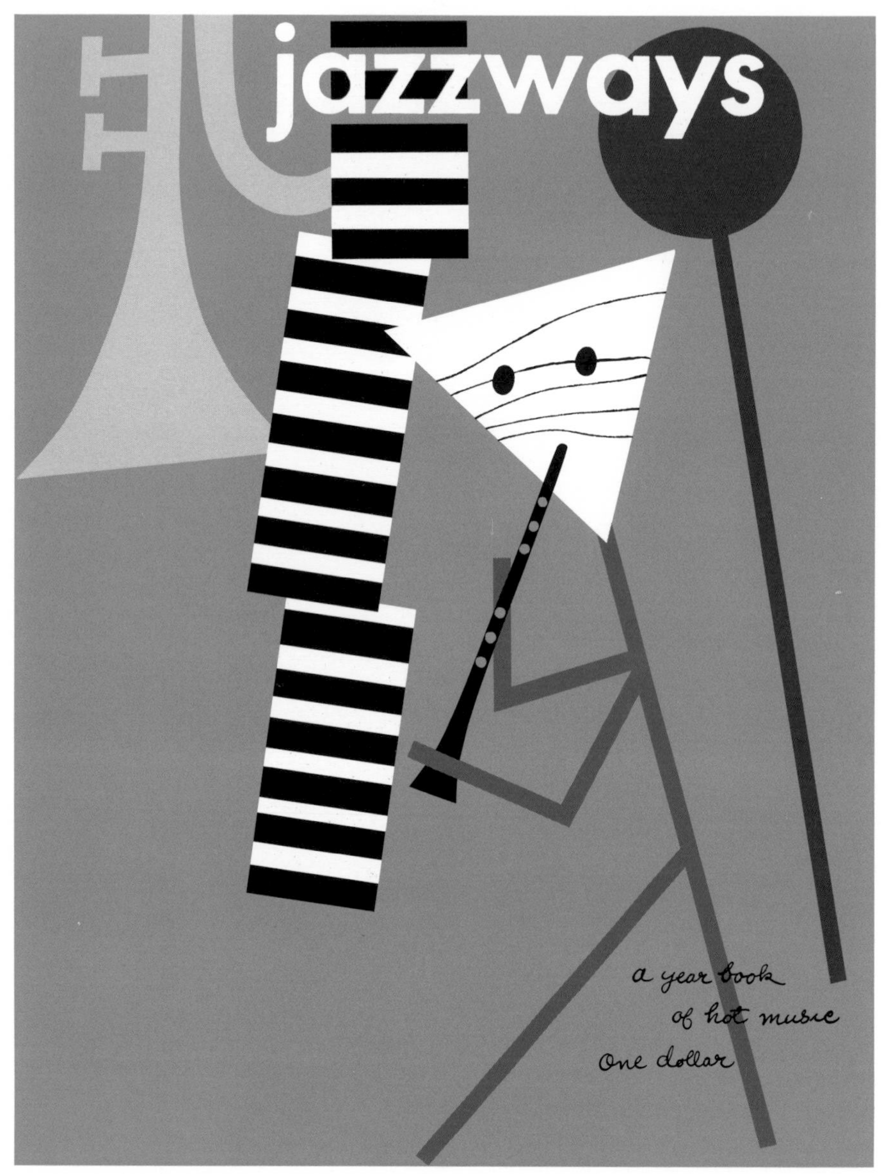

ollage nd Montage

It is a truism that the fundamental problem of the advertiser and publisher is to get the message into the reader's mind. Commonplace images and unimaginative visualization afford the spectator little reason to become engrossed in an advertiser's product. Radio and television advertisers, who use media by which it is possible for studio and home spectators to take part in the proceedings, have discovered the value of audience participation. Producers of print advertising, on the other hand, must devise methods of engaging the eye and attention of the reader in a manner consistent with the printed form. Picture puzzles, cryptograms, quizzes, memory tests, and teaser devices have been employed to this end from time to time.

Contemporary graphic design techniques, resulting from experiments and discoveries in the fields of psychology, art, and science, suggest many possibilities. Among the great contributions to visual thought is the invention of collage. Collage and montage permit the integration of seemingly unrelated objects or ideas in a single picture; they enable the designer to indicate simultaneous events or scenes which by more conventional methods would result in a series of isolated pictures. The complex message presented in a single picture more readily enables the spectator to focus his attention on the advertiser's message.

Contemporary as it may seem, the concept of simultaneity takes us back to ancient China. The Chinese, aware of the need for a means of expressing in one picture simultaneous actions or multiple events, devised a form of oblique projection. They also devised a means of showing one object behind, above, or below another by free disposition of elements in a composition, completely disregarding the illusions of visual perspective. This was essentially a method of formalizing or neutralizing the object. It was a transformation resulting in formal arrangements rather than conventional illustration. In one sense montage and collage are integrated visual arrangements in space, and in another sense they are absorbing visual tests that the spectator may perceive and decipher for himself. He may thus participate directly in the creative process.

Annual Report cover,
Westinghouse Electric Corporation,
1970

Advertisement, Penn/Brite papers,
New York & Pennsylvania Company,
1964

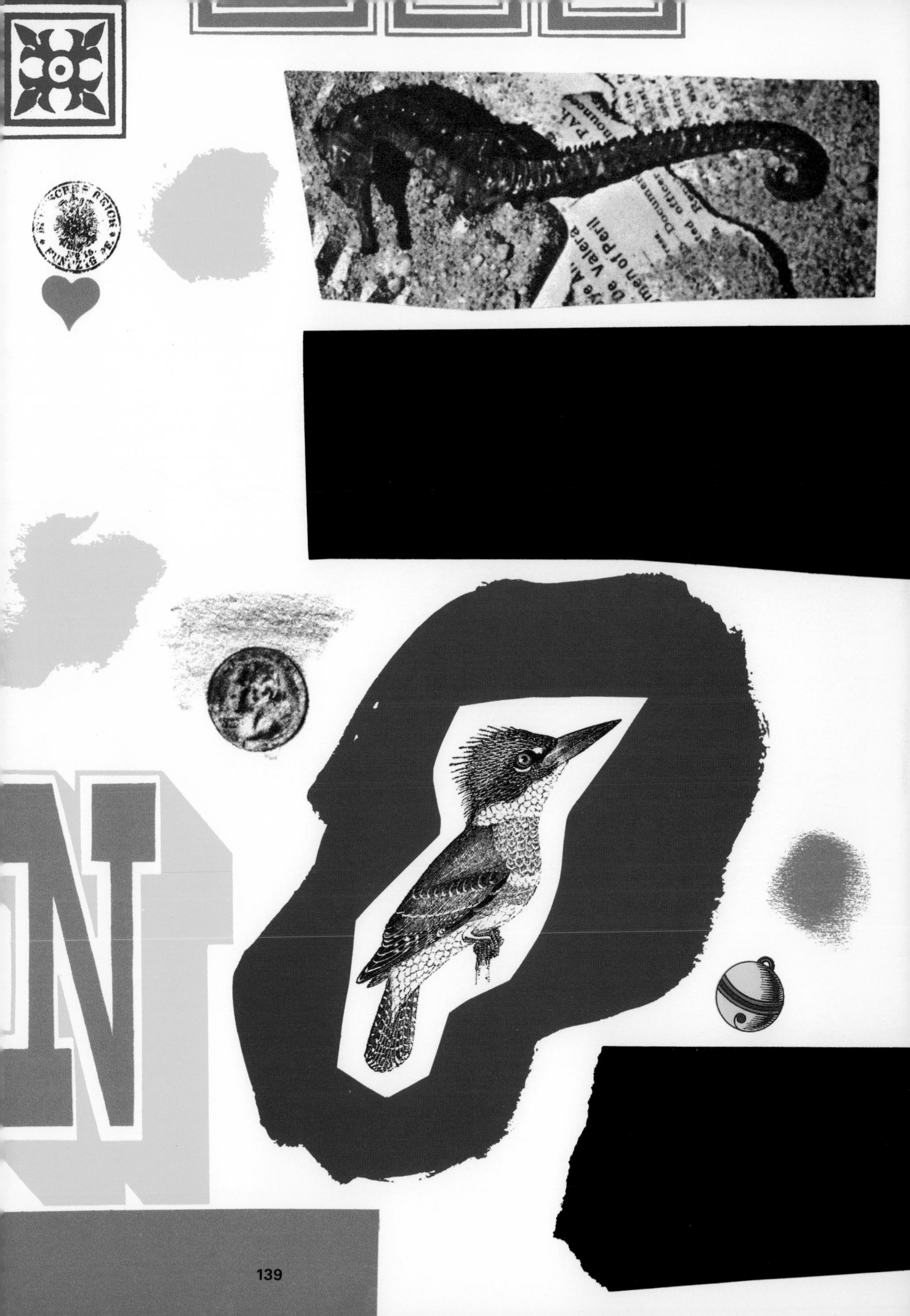

Folder,
IBM Corporation,
1978

Label designs,
Schenley Distillers Inc.,
1942

SCHENLEY
CLUB
Distilled London dry Gin
DISTILLED
FROM 100%
AMERICAN GRAINS
LAWRENCEBURG, INDIANA

SCHENLEY
94.8
Distilled London Dry
GIN
94.8 Proof
4/5 quart
DISTILLED FROM 100% AMERICAN GRAINS
BY SCHENLEY DISTILLERIES, INC., LAWRENCEBURG, IND.

In this 1953 Olivetti advertisement the juxtaposition of objects and visual techniques are in contrast.

Yesterday and Today

Disputes arising between the two schools of typographic thought, the *traditional* on the one hand and the *modern* on the other are, it seems to me, the fruits of misplaced emphasis. I believe the real difference lies in the way space is interpreted: that is, the way in which an image is placed on a sheet of paper. Such incidental questions as the use of sans-serif typefaces, lowercase letters, ragged settings, primary colors, etc., are at best variables that tend merely to sidetrack the real issue.

"But great original artists," says John Dewey, "take a tradition into themselves. They have not shunned but digested it. Then the very conflict set up between it and what is new in themselves and in their environment creates the tension that demands a new mode of expression."[1] Understanding modern and traditional in this light, the designer is able to bring together in a new and logical relationship traditional graphic forms and ideas and "new" concepts based on a contemporary point of view. This union of two supposedly divergent forces provides conditions that lead to fresh visual experiences.

1 John Dewey, "The Natural History of Form," *Art as Experience* (New York, 1934), 159.

In advertising one is often faced with the problem of conveying a quality of age. In the example that follows, traditional ornaments combine with geometric forms to establish new relationships. This transition from old to new may be accomplished by arranging these familiar devices in some surprising manner.

This transition from old to new may be effected by unorthodox arrangement of "traditional forms."

Brochure cover,
IBM Corporation,
1964

Label design,
Dubonnet Corporation,
1942

SWEET
VERMOUTH
by Dubonnet
PRODUCT OF USA

Magazine advertisement,
Disney Hats,
1946

Annual Report,
Cummins Engine Company,
1962

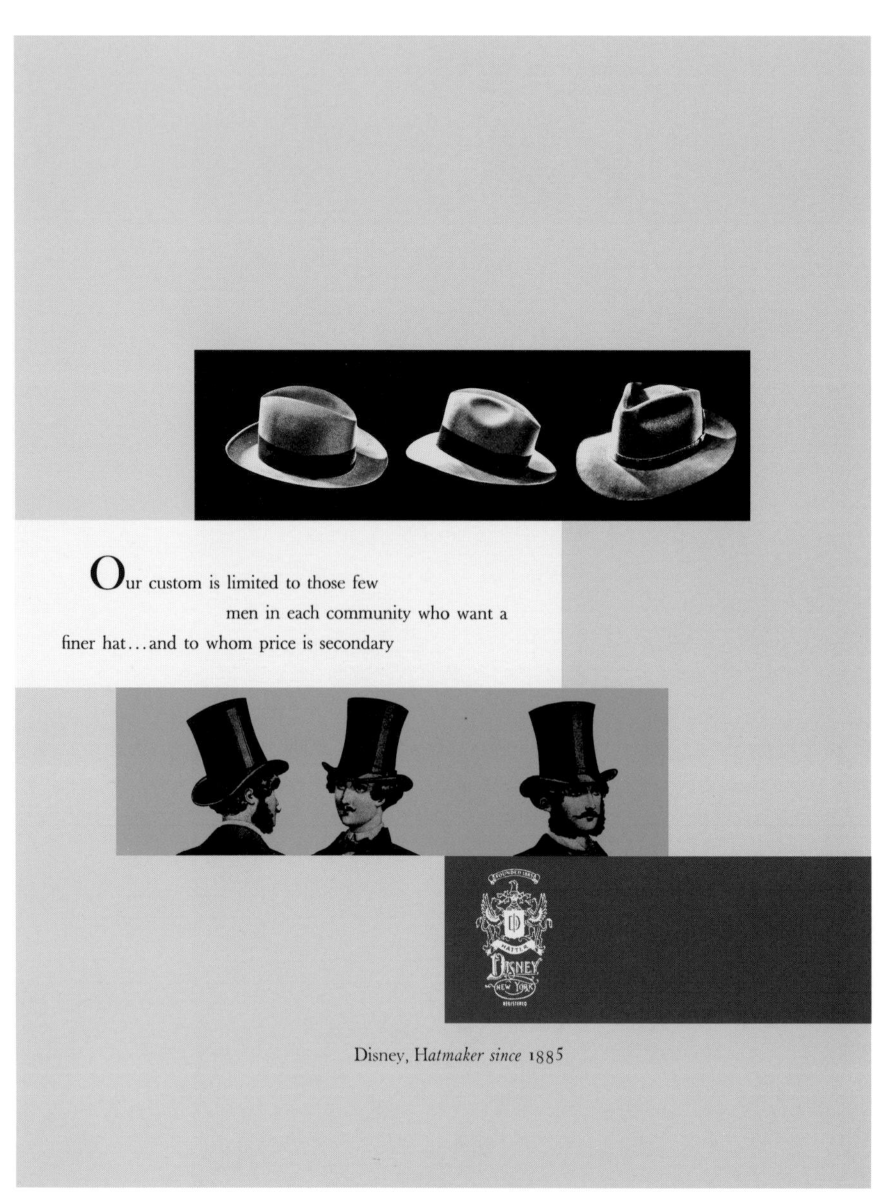

Our custom is limited to those few
men in each community who want a
finer hat... and to whom price is secondary
DISNEY
NEW YORK
HATTERS
Disney, *Hatmaker since* 1885

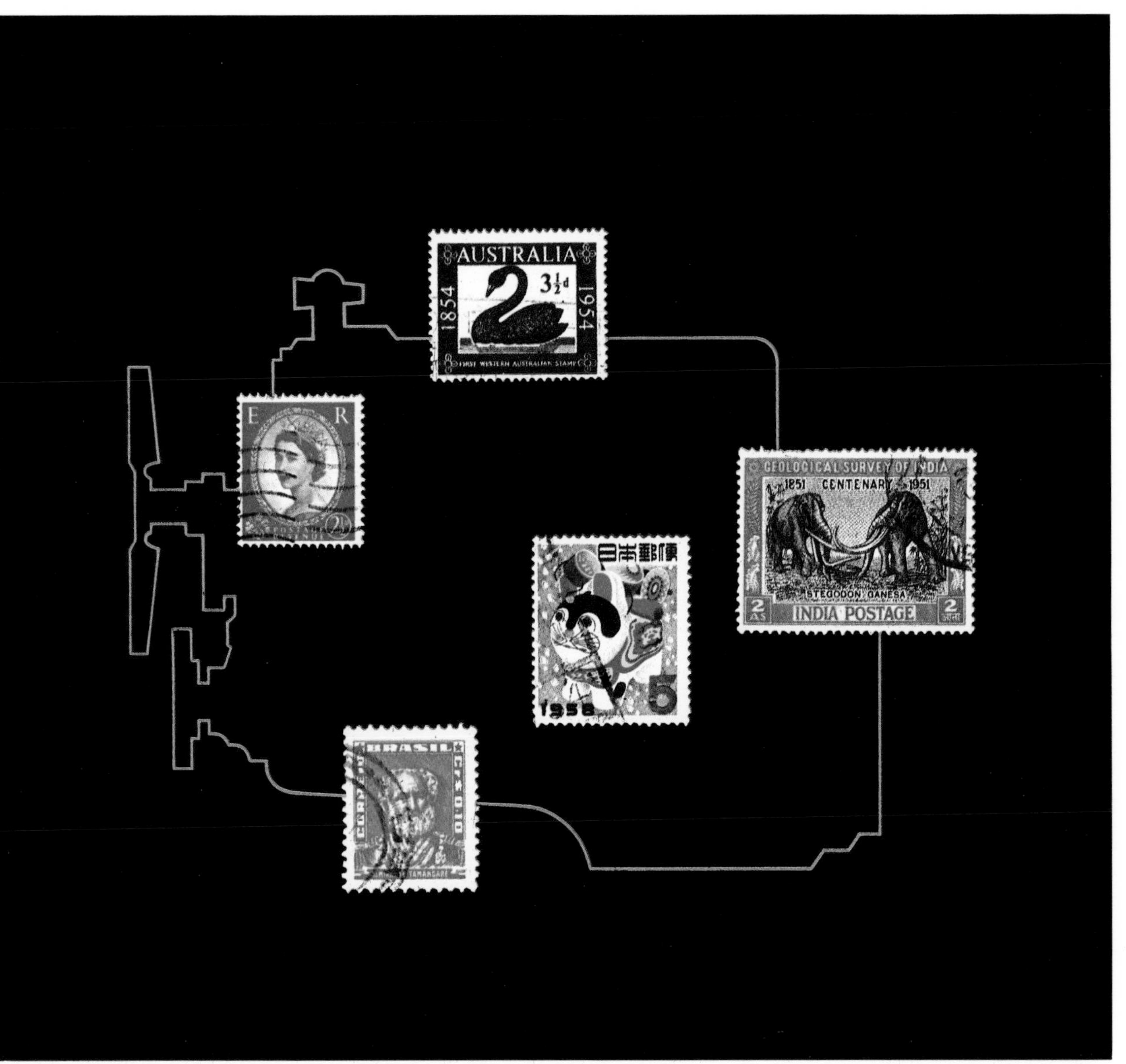
AUSTRALIA
3½d
1854
1954
FIRST WESTERN AUSTRALIAN STAMP
E R
GEOLOGICAL SURVEY OF INDIA
1851 CENTENARY 1951
STEGODON GANESA
2
INDIA POSTAGE
2
日本郵便
5
BRASIL

Typographic Form and Expression

One of the objectives of the designer who deals with type matter involves readability. Unfortunately, however, this function is often taken too literally and overemphasized at the expense of style, individuality, and the very effectiveness of the printed piece itself. By carefully arranging type areas, spacing, size, and color, the typographer is able to impart to the printed page a quality that helps to dramatize the contents. He is able to translate type matter into tactile patterns. By concentrating the type area and emphasizing the margin (white space), he can reinforce, by contrast, the textural quality of the type. The resulting effect on the reader may be properly compared to the sensation produced by physical contact with metal type.

45 years go to work for victory
From its very inception in 1897 every Autocar activity has trained the Company for its vital role in the war program. For 45 years without interruption it has manufactured motor vehicles exclusively, concentrating in the last decade on heavy-duty trucks of 5 tons or over. For 45 years Autocar has pioneered the way, developing many history-making "firsts" in the industry: the first porcelain spark-plug; the first American shaft-driven automobile; the first double reduction gear drive; the first

circulating oil system. For 45 years Autocar insistence on mechanical perfection has wrought a tradition of precision that is honored by every one of its master workers. These are achievements that only time can win. The harvest of these years, of this vast experience, is at the service of our government. Autocar is meeting its tremendous responsibility to national defense by putting its 45 years' experience to work in helping to build for America a motorized armada such as the world has never seen.

Brochure,
The Autocar Corporation,
1942

Book illustration,
Listen! Listen!
Harcourt Brace & World,
1970

Rrroooaaarrrrr!

How do I love thee ? Let me count the ways.

I love thee to the depth and breadth and height

My soul can reach, when feeling out of sight

For the ends of Being and ideal Grace.

I love thee to the level of every day's

Most quiet need, by sun and candle-light.

I lo th fre as me st fo Ri

Keepsake,
Pastore DePamphilis Rampone, Inc.,
1984

e ee rely, ey n m aise.

I love thee with the passion put to use

In my old griefs, and with my child-hood's faith.

I love thee with a love I seemed to lose

With my lost saints, — I love thee with the breath,

Smiles, tears, of all my life! — and, if God choose,

I shall but love thee better after death.

Binding, jacket, and book design,
Alfred A. Knopf,
1945

Genesis: 3

The Bible, since the days of Gutenberg,
has been an inspiration to typographers of many lands.
The text of this interpretation is from
the translation issued by the Jewish Publication
Society of America in 1917.

1. Now the serpent was more subtle than any beast
of the field which the Lord God had made. And
he said unto the woman: 'Yea, hath God said:
Ye shall not eat of any tree of the garden?'
2. And the woman said unto the serpent: 'Of the
fruit of the trees of the garden we may eat;
3. but of the fruit of the tree which is in the midst of
the garden, God hath said: Ye shall not eat of
it, neither shall ye touch it, lest ye die.'
4. And the serpent said unto the woman: 'Ye shall
not surely die;
5. for God doth know that in the day ye eat thereof,
then your eyes shall be opened, and ye shall be
as God, knowing good and evil.'

6. And when the woman saw that the tree
for food, and that it was a delight to the
and that the tree was to be desired to m
wise, she took of the fruit thereof, and d
and she gave also unto her husband wit
he did eat.
7. And the eyes of them both were opened
they knew that they were naked; and th
figleaves together, and made themselve
8. And they heard the voice of the Lord G
walking in the garden toward the cool c
and the man and his wife hid themselve
the presence of the Lord God amongst
of the garden.

nd the Lord God called unto the man, and said
nto him: 'Where art thou?'
nd he said: 'I heard Thy voice in the garden,
nd I was afraid, because I was naked; and I hid
nyself.'
nd He said: 'Who told thee that thou wast
aked? Hast thou eaten of the tree, whereof
commanded thee that thou shouldest not eat?'
nd the man said: 'The woman whom Thou
avest to be with me, she gave me of the tree,
nd I did eat.'
nd the Lord God said unto the woman: 'What
s this thou hast done?' And the woman said:
he serpent beguiled me, and I did eat.'

14. And the Lord God said unto the serpent:
'Because thou hast done this, cursed art thou
from among all cattle, and from among all beasts
of the field; upon thy belly shalt thou go, and
dust shalt thou eat all the days of thy life.
15. And I will put enmity between thee and the
woman, and between thy seed and her seed; they
shall bruise thy head, and thou shalt bruise
their heel.'
16. Unto the woman He said: 'I will greatly
multiply thy pain and thy travail; in pain thou
shalt bring forth children; and thy desire shall
be to thy husband, and he shall rule over thee.'

17. And unto Adam He said: 'Because thou hast
hearkened unto the voice of thy wife, and hast
eaten of the tree, of which I commanded
thee, saying: Thou shalt not eat of it; cursed is
the ground for thy sake; in toil shalt thou eat
of it all the days of thy life.
18. Thorns also and thistles shall it bring forth to
thee; and thou shalt eat the herb of the field.
19. In the sweat of thy face shalt thou eat bread, till
thou return unto the ground; for out of it wast
thou taken; for dust thou art, and unto dust shalt
thou return.'
20. And the man called his wife's name Eve; because
she was the mother of all living.

21. And the Lord God made for Adam and for his
wife garments of skins, and clothed them.
22. And the Lord God said: 'Behold, the man is
become as one of us, to know good and evil; and
now, lest he put forth his hand, and take also
of the tree of life, and eat, and live for ever.'
23. Therefore the Lord God sent him forth from the
garden of Eden, to till the ground from whence
he was taken.
24. So He drove out the man; and He placed at
the east of the garden of Eden the cherubim, and
the flaming sword which turned every way, to
keep the way to the tree of life.

Design and typography: Paul Rand
Composition and offset printing: Tri-Arts Press
Text: 14 Linotype Garamond #3
Paper: Clear Spring Book, antique offset natural

Cover design,
Design Quarterly,
1984

Advertisement,
Disney Hats,
1946

1. Roger Fry, "Sensibility," *Last Lectures* (London, 1939), 22.

With asymmetric balance, he is able to achieve greater interest. Bilateral symmetry offers the spectator too simple and too obvious a statement. It offers little or no intellectual pleasure, no challenge. For the pleasure derived from observing asymmetric arrangements lies partly in overcoming resistances which, consciously or not, the spectator has in his own mind, and in thus acquiring some sort of aesthetic satisfaction. (For a more comprehensive discussion along these lines, see Roger Fry's essay "Sensibility.")[1]

In ordering the space and in distributing his typographic material and symbols, the designer is able to predetermine, to a certain degree, the eye movements of the spectator.

Disney, Hatmaker since 1885
Mr. Disney's
custom is limited to those few men
in each community who
want a finer hat . . . and to whom
price is secondary

*Advertisement,
Stafford Fabrics,
1944*

fabrics with a pedigree . . .
fabrics stafford
from the Stafford stallion . . .
symbol of those famous Stafford fabrics . . .
loomed in Pennsylvania, printed
in the little Connecticut town
for which they are named
GOODMAN & THEISE, INC.
16 East 34th Street, New York 16, N. Y.
Stafford Springs, Conn., Scranton, Pa.

Annual Report,
Cummins Engine Company,
1967

Cummins Custom Torque engines maintain maximum speeds while reducing shifts.

Cummins standby generator sets assure against electrical power failure in major building complexes.

Backhoes, excavators, and cranes are significant new markets for Cummins compact V diesels.

This unique four-wheel drive farm tractor powered by a Cummins compact V diesel tills the soil.

A Cummins industrial power unit and this balloon remove logs from remote timber areas.

Sightseers at Niagara Falls enjoy a tour aboard the Cummins powered Maid of the Mist II.

Cummins compact v6 and v8 diesels are gaining wide acceptance in intercity hauling operations.

A typeface that sometimes is described as having *character* is often merely bizarre, eccentric, nostalgic, or simply buckeye.

To distort the letters of the alphabet in the style of Chinese calligraphy (sometimes referred to as chop suey lettering) because the subject happens to deal with the Orient is to create the typographic equivalent of a corny illustration. To mimic a woodcut style of type to go with a woodcut; to use bold type to harmonize with heavy machinery, etc., is clichéd thinking. The designer is unaware of the exciting possibilities inherent in the *contrast* of picture and type matter. Thus, instead of combining a woodcut with a harmonious type style (Neuland), a happier choice would be a more familiar design (Caslon, Bodoni, or Helvetica) to achieve the element of surprise and to accentuate by contrast the form and character of both text and picture.

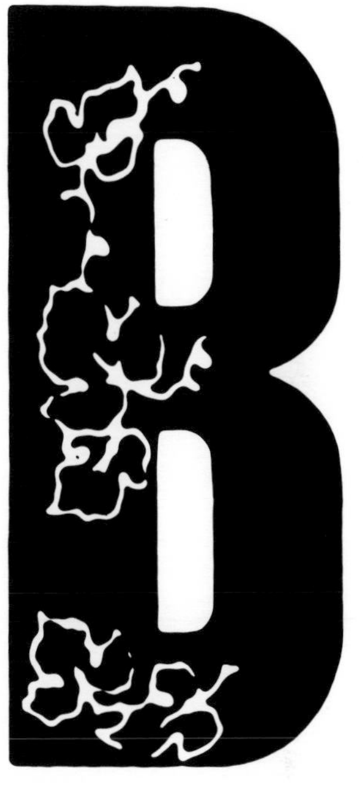

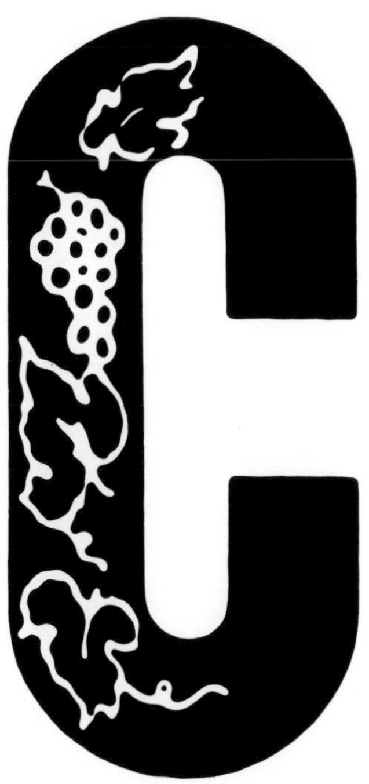

Two letters from a Cresta Blanca Wine logotype (1943) demonstrate how the simple addition of ornament changes a commonplace letter (associated more with bold newspaper headlines than with delicate vintage wines) to a memorable image. Here, contrast plays a significant role.

Advertisement,
Smith, Kline & French Laboratories,
1943

"Some Griefs Are Medicinable"

...Cymbeline act III, scene II

Many patients
stricken with grief
over misfortune
or bereavement develop
abnormal reactive
depressions... differentiated
from normal
depressions of mood by
their inordinate
intensity and stubborn
persistence.
With these patients,
Benzedrine Sulfate therapy
is often dramatically
effective.
In many cases,

benzedrine sulfate

will break the
vicious circle of
depression,
renew the patient's
interest and optimism,
and restore his
capacity for physical
and mental effort.

Smith, Kline & French Laboratories,

By contrasting type and pictorial matter, the designer is able to create new combinations and elicit new meanings. For instance, in the Air-Wick newspaper advertisement, the old and the new are brought into harmony by contrasting two apparently unrelated subjects—nineteenth-century wood engravings and twentieth-century typewriter type.

The surrounding white space helps to separate the advertisement from its competitors, creates an illusion of greater size per square inch, and produces a sense of cleanliness and freshness.

Advertisement,
Seeman Brothers, Air-Wick,
1944

The numeral as a means of expression possesses many of the same qualities as the letter. It can also be the visual equivalent of time, space, position, and quantity; and it can help to impart to a printed piece a sense of rhythm and immediacy.

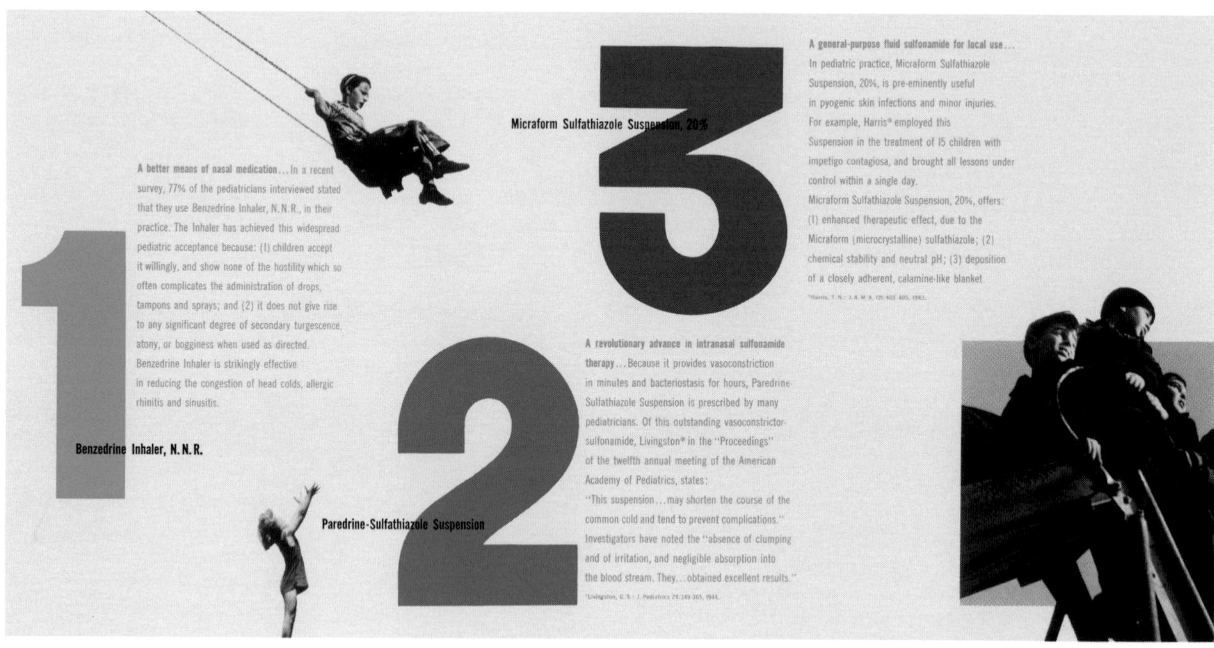

1
A better means of nasal medication... In a recent survey, 77% of the pediatricians interviewed stated that they use Benzedrine Inhaler, N.N.R., in their practice. The Inhaler has achieved this widespread pediatric acceptance because: (1) children accept it willingly, and show none of the hostility which so often complicates the administration of drops, tampons and sprays; and (2) it does not give rise to any significant degree of secondary turgescence, atony, or bogginess when used as directed. Benzedrine Inhaler is strikingly effective in reducing the congestion of head colds, allergic rhinitis and sinusitis.
Benzedrine Inhaler, N.N.R.
2
Paredrine-Sulfathiazole Suspension
A revolutionary advance in intranasal sulfonamide therapy... Because it provides vasoconstriction in minutes and bacteriostasis for hours, Paredrine-Sulfathiazole Suspension is prescribed by many pediatricians. Of this outstanding vasoconstrictor-sulfonamide, Livingston* in the "Proceedings" of the twelfth annual meeting of the American Academy of Pediatrics, states: "This suspension...may shorten the course of the common cold and tend to prevent complications." Investigators have noted the "absence of clumping and of irritation, and negligible absorption into the blood stream. They...obtained excellent results."
*Livingston, G. S.: J. Pediatrics 24:349-365, 1944.
3
Micraform Sulfathiazole Suspension, 20%
A general-purpose fluid sulfonamide for local use... In pediatric practice, Micraform Sulfathiazole Suspension, 20%, is pre-eminently useful in pyogenic skin infections and minor injuries. For example, Harris* employed this Suspension in the treatment of 15 children with impetigo contagiosa, and brought all lessons under control within a single day.
Micraform Sulfathiazole Suspension, 20%, offers: (1) enhanced therapeutic effect, due to the Micraform (microcrystalline) sulfathiazole; (2) chemical stability and neutral pH; (3) deposition of a closely adherent, calamine-like blanket.

Prospectus,
Smith, Kline & French Laboratories,
1945

Poster,
New York Art Directors Club,
1963

design 63

*Cover design,
A. D. Magazine,
1941*

*Magazine cover,
Direction,
1945*

The isolated letter affords a means of visual expression that other kinds of imagery cannot quite duplicate. Letters in the forms of trademarks, seals, and monograms—on business forms, identification tags, athletic jerseys, and even handkerchiefs—possess some magical quality. They serve not only as status symbols but have the virtue of brevity as well.

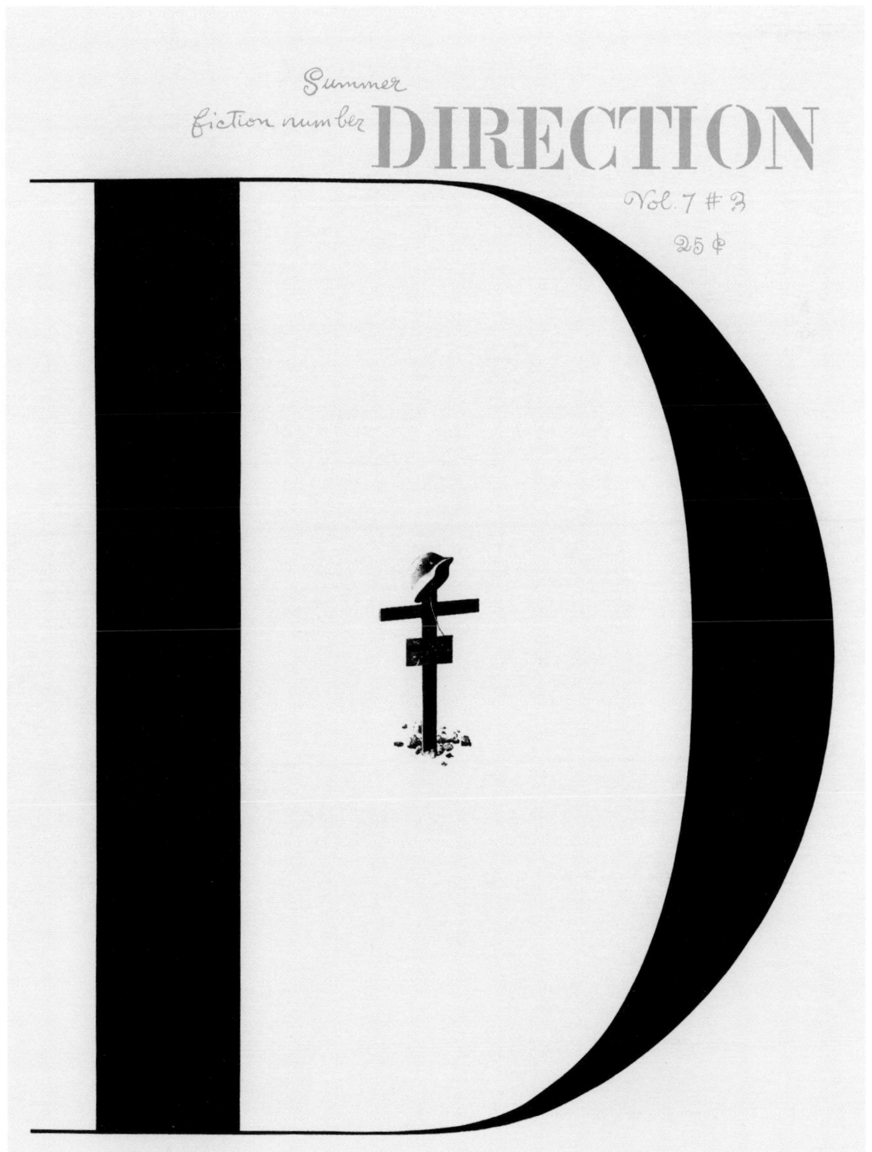

*Magazine covers,
Direction,
1941*

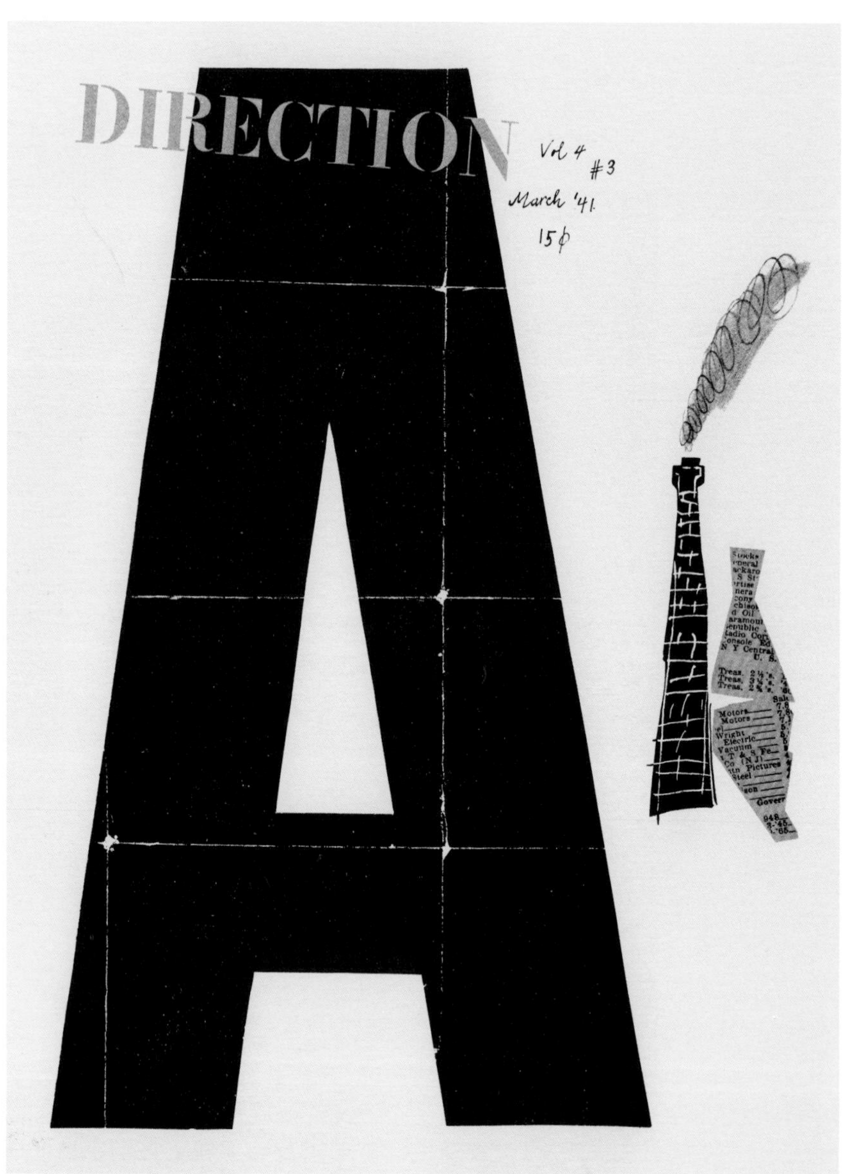

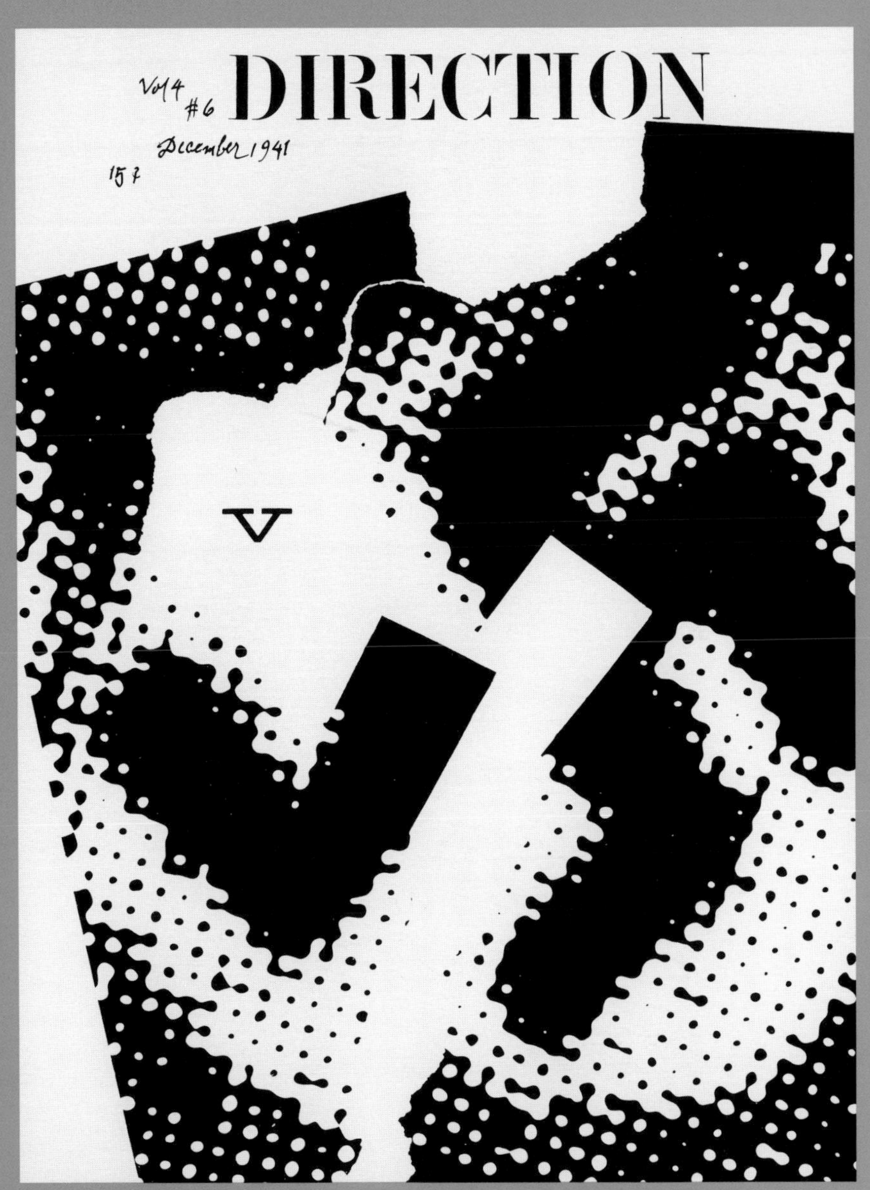
Vol 4 #6
DIRECTION
December 1941
15¢
V

Resource Management:
Energy and
Materials Conservation
Ridesharing
Environment Protection
IBM

Poster,
IBM Corporation,
1980

Punctuation marks, as emotive, plastic symbols, have served the artist as a means of expression in paintings as well as in the applied arts.

Jacket design, Alfred A. Knopf, 1945

Magazine cover,
Direction,
1940

Booklet,
Coordinator of Inter American Affairs,
1943

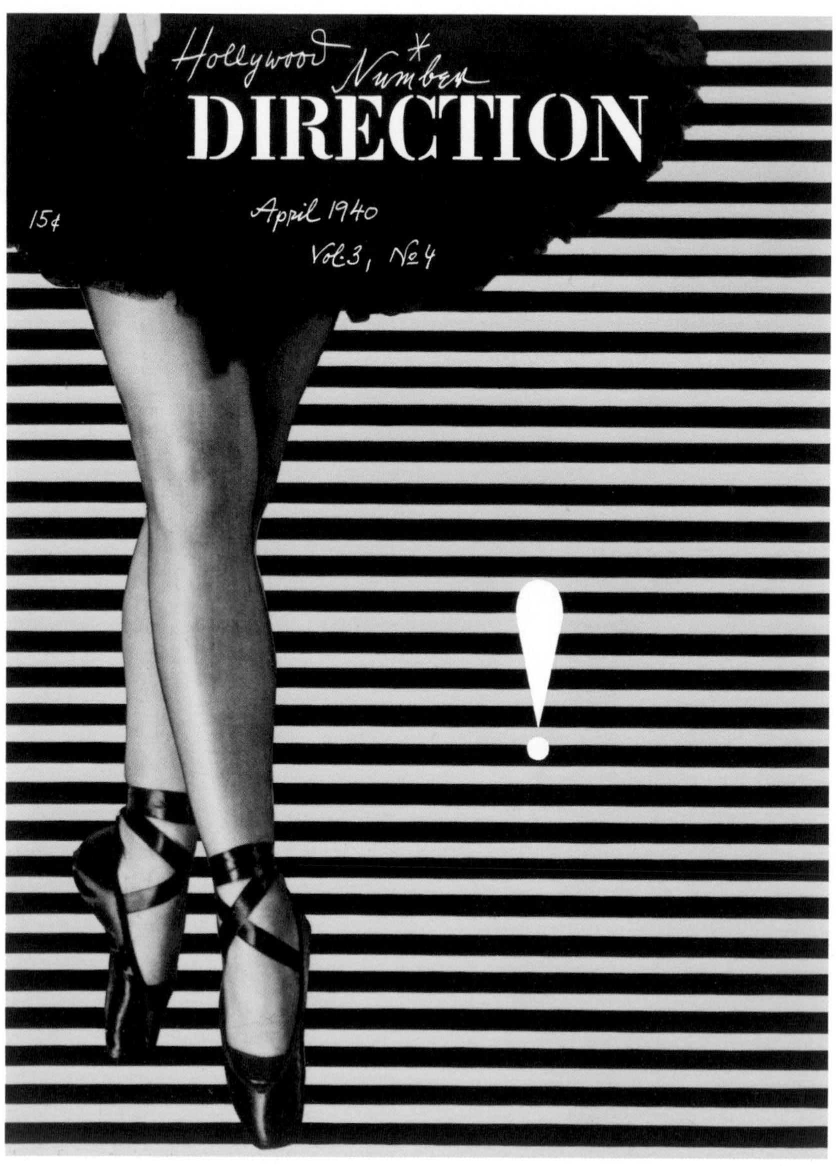

Coco, mostraram, aos fazendeiros, o primeiro arado que, jamais, viram. No futuro, as refeições, destes fazendeiros, serão melhores.

Os Homens:

Estes variados planos que dizem respeito à saude, reconstrução e alimèntação, são orientados por homens competentes, cujas funções variam, desde as negociações com o governo, até a edificação de hospitais de seis andares; desde da montagem de mosquiteiros à organização da indústria da fibra; desde o trabalho de exterminar ratos, por meio de lança-chamas, à construção de acampamentos para trabalhadores.

Os homens, que realizam este mister, devem saber como enfrentar terremotos, incêndios, enchentes, secas, cobras, pulgas, arraias venenosas, peixes elétricos, vampiros, formigas carnívoras . . . e a propaganda nazista.

Entre estes profissionais, se encontram diplomatas, contadores, sanitaristas, economistas, engenheiros sanitaristas, especialistas em medicina tropical, enfermeiras e fazendeiros, cujo objetivo é proporcionar um padrão de vida mais elevado, para todas as Américas.

Em uma palavra, o objetivo, destes pioneiros e colaboradores, é estabelecer ambiente social em que o simples cidadão, irritado com meras palavras, possa conseguir uma refeição substancial, quando faminto, e cuidado médico, quando doente; sim, um ambiente social em que todos vivamos uma vida digna de ser vivida. **O Homen, Quanto Vale?**

...Para nós, nas vinte e uma repúblicas da América, êle vale tudo !

Things
we know about
tomorrow:

A new Westinghouse development could be your heart's best friend!

It is a little electronic device with the unlikely name of "Cardiac Pacer." Originally, it was developed to provide a gentle boost to a patient whose heart faltered or stopped during an operation, or for use as a heart stimulant in hospital recovery rooms.
Now Westinghouse is working to perfect it for personal use on millions of heart patients by their physicians. It would be light and easy to carry about. It may not be cheap, but then life is worth a lot to any of us.
Part of the plan for the future is a radio receiver about the size of a pack of cigarettes which a doctor could carry with him and, if any of his heart patients had any trouble, the radio would beep-beep the doctor. He could then tune in to that patient, listen to his heart beats, if necessary, and advise emergency treatment. Wondrous are the uses of electricity.

You can be sure ... if it's Westinghouse

About Legibility

In a survey made by Clark University in 1911 to ascertain "the relative legibility of different faces of printing types," twenty-six faces of widely dissimilar designs were studied, among which were Caslon, Century, Cheltenham, and News Gothic. "Ye gods! and has it come to this?" was the reaction of F. W. Goudy, the prolific type designer, to the results of the survey, which judged News Gothic to be "the nearest approximation of an ideal face."[1] This tidbit appeared in Mr. Goudy's *Typologia,* published in 1940 by the University of California Press. Prejudice is not the only virtue of this book. In fact, I found it utterly absorbing and hope that the reader's curiosity is sufficiently aroused to look it up.

1 *Typologia,* p. 142.

Equally revealing, although sprinkled here and there with a number of miscellaneous ideas with which it is difficult to agree, is Stanley Morison's little book *First Principles of Typography* (Macmillan, 1936). In referring to the design of the title page, Morison dogmatically states: "As lower case is a necessary evil, which we should do well to subordinate since we cannot suppress, it should be avoided when it is at its least rational and least attractive—in larger sizes."[2] And the discriminating reader will note both the sense and nonsense of the following: "The main line of a title should be set in capitals and, *like all capitals, should be spaced.*" The first part of this statement is, of course, clearly controversial; the italicized part is true most of the time, but not all of the time.

2 *First Principles,* p. 19.

Both books, however, are full of scholarly, useful, and occasionally amusing information. I say useful because they spell out those aspects of type design and typography that have little to do with trendiness and that instead deal with those unchanging, timeless qualities of good design.

Before leaving this very brief reference to legibility, it is well to remember that behavior patterns, habit, and familiarity with a particular typeface seriously influence the judgment of the designer and his audience in matters of style, type selection, and readability. Both Messrs. Goudy and Morison have demonstrated that typographic objectivity is next to impossible. It is clear that taste, prejudice, trends, popularity polls, and the foibles of the marketplace play some sort of role in affecting one's typographic judgment.

Title pages:

Museum of Modern Art, 1948

Wittenborn, Schultz, Inc., 1948

Art Institute of Chicago, 1949

Paintings, drawings,

and prints

by Paul K*lee*

from the Klee Foundation, Berne, Switzerland

with additions from American collections

The Museum of Modern Art, New York

\+

Cincinnati Museum Association

Detroit Institute of Arts

Portland Art Museum, Portland, Oregon

City Art Museum of St. Louis

San Francisco Museum of Art

Phillips Gallery, Washington, D.C.

The Documents of Modern Art. *Director, Robert Motherwell*

a r p

On My Way *poetry and essays* 1912...1947

Wittenborn, Schultz, Inc., New York, 1948

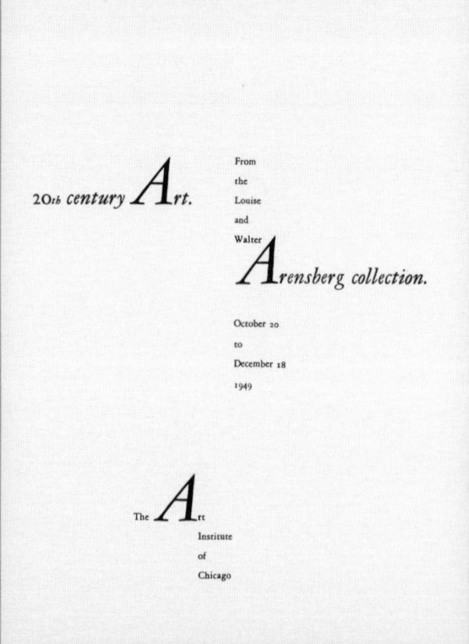

20th century Art.

From the Louise and Walter *Arensberg collection.*

October 20 to December 18 1949

The Art Institute of Chicago

Annual Report,
IBM Corporation,
1977

in San Jose, Calif. During the year, 16 major IBM facilities were completed or under construction in the U.S. and 13 abroad. We increased the IBM employee population worldwide to more than 310,000, from 292,000 at the start of 1977.

Tax and Trade Issues

The current proposal to repeal the present system of U.S. taxation of foreign earnings would put U.S. corporations operating overseas at a serious disadvantage by raising their tax costs significantly relative to foreign competitors. Today, no foreign government imposes such tax handicaps on its own companies competing abroad. In fact, most foreign governments help those companies in a variety of ways, even including direct subsidies. Restrictive U.S. tax measures not only make American companies less competitive, they also reduce U.S. jobs that depend on exports.

IBM and many other businesses have a great deal riding on the success of the current negotiations under the auspices of the General Agreement on Tariffs and Trade (GATT) that would reduce both tariff and non-tariff trade barriers. Some 40 countries have duty rates on data processing equipment at least twice as high as those of the U.S.—a disparity that we hope the GATT negotiations will reduce.

Changes in Operations Overseas

In November, 1977, after repeated efforts to reach an understanding with the Indian government, which had required us to give up 60% ownership of our business there, we felt we had no choice but to change our mode of operations.

We believe that in a high-technology, rapidly developing industry such as ours, the necessary worldwide coordination of research, development, manufacturing, sales and service can best be carried out with full ownership of subsidiaries. In discussions with the Indian government over a long period, we believed that a mutually acceptable resolution would be found. Unfortunately, this did not come to pass, and we have accordingly phased out our Bombay plant and will phase out our marketing and maintenance operations in India by mid-1978.

Subject to the approval of the Indian government, we will maintain a limited presence in India by establishing a liaison office where we can receive authorized requests for our products and services.

We were able to reach an agreement in principle with Indonesia in December, 1977, that will enable us to continue offering our products and services. An Indonesian law specified that foreign companies must turn their trading activities over to Indonesians by the end of 1977. Our agreement included the appointment of an agent to trade on our behalf, as well as reorganization of our operation so as to maintain a presence there. We look forward to continued business activity in Indonesia.

The Lawsuits

The U.S. Justice Department's antitrust suit against IBM went to trial in May, 1975, and so far only the government has presented its case. We expect to start our defense by mid-1978 and will need considerable time to present our side.

In February, 1977, the Federal District Court hearing antitrust charges brought against IBM by California Computer Products, Inc., dismissed the action at the close of Calcomp's presentation of its case. The court ordered a directed verdict in favor of IBM. Calcomp is appealing that decision.

The U.S. Court of Appeals has granted Greyhound Computer Corporation's petition for a new trial. In July, 1972, Greyhound's antitrust charges against IBM were dismissed before IBM had presented its defense.

Trial of the antitrust suit by Memorex Corporation commenced in January, 1978.

We are convinced that we have achieved our business position through fair and ethical competition and that our legal position is sound in each case. Further details on these and other lawsuits are contained in the financial section of this report.

Repurchase of IBM Stock

In February, 1977, we made a stock tender offer and repurchased more than 2½ million shares of our own stock. In July, the Board of Directors authorized the purchase from time to time of additional large blocks of capital stock. Over the last six months of 1977, we purchased about 694,000 additional shares. All of the shares purchased in this way have been canceled and restored to the status of authorized but unissued shares.

For the Future

Looking ahead, we see a sound business environment over the long term. We are in a young, expanding business, one that is clearly needed by society. We believe IBM is in a position to respond to the very large potential in information processing in many countries throughout the world.

IBM's achievements in 1977 reflect the creativity and hard work of IBM people in the many countries where we operate. We are deeply grateful for their skill and dedication. They are our best assurance of continuing growth for IBM and its business in the years ahead.

January 31, 1978
by order of the Board of Directors

Frank T. Cary
Chairman of the Board

John R. Opel
President

Information working for people...

At one time, customers used IBM products for only a few information-handling tasks—such as inventory and payroll or scientific study—out of the public sight.

Today, information technology in some form is visible almost everywhere. It is touching people's lives directly. It provides ease of buying through terminals in department stores, faster checkout at supermarket counters, or 24-hour banking at sidewalk teller machines.

Moreover, the information being handled is taking many forms besides the letters and numbers still processed today in most applications. More and more, the information is encompassing a broader spectrum of timely data. The strength of a human pulse monitored by computer may be critically important information for the doctor working against time. Pressure fluctuations in a natural gas line can be vital information in assuring heat and power for homes and industry. Amid the growing complexities of modern life, information in its multiple forms is becoming a fundamental resource for societies around the world.

Whatever those forms, machine systems are needed to collect the information and to store, process, retrieve and communicate it quickly and accurately to the end user. Providing such systems is IBM's business. IBM's many products, from computers to copiers, are assisting customers in all parts of the world to process information in manufacturing, banking, distribution, health care, science and engineering, government, entertainment and many other aspects of daily living.

Shown on the following pages are some of the ways IBM customers are putting information to work, as well as ways IBM people and new products are helping to make that work more efficient and productive.

"The Good Old Neue Typografie"

In 1959 in a paper titled *Typography U.S.A.*, the Type Director's Club announced: "At last a new form... an entirely new concept in typography has been realized, a typography that is purely American. This new typography, the product of contemporary science, industry, art, and technology, has become recognized internationally as the 'New American Typography'!"

In the light of what has happened and what is happening in this field in America, it is very difficult for me to understand this claim. This is not to say that the statement is deliberately misleading, but merely that I, personally, am unaware that anything of the sort is occurring.

The writer goes on to ask: "What is this new form?" My response: I don't know. And to the next question: "What does it look like?" I can only say that the best of it looks like typography that could have come from Germany, Switzerland, England, Holland, or France. Briefly, it is an offspring of the International Style, which means not only a blending of the ideas of different peoples but an interaction of the different arts – painting, architecture and poetry: the poetry of Mallarmé, the ideograms of Apollinaire, the collages of Picasso and Braque, the montages of Hartfield and Schwitters, the paintings of Doesburg and Léger, the architecture of Oud and Le Corbusier.

To deny the fact that American typography is basically a continuation of, sometimes a retrogradation from, and sometimes an improvement upon the "new typography" which was nurtured on the continent of Europe, is to ignore the revolutionary impact of Cubism, Dadaism, and all the other "isms" of the early twentieth century. It is also to overlook the influence of movements such as *de Stijl*, the ideas of the Bauhaus, and the contributions of those who changed the face of traditional typography.

There is little question but that such a thing as American illustration or even American automobile or refrigerator design exists. Whatever their merits, they are American, not Americanized. On the other hand, I believe the New American Typography can more accurately be called the New Americanized European Typography, given its origins.

This is not to say that individual American designers have not made valuable contributions to typographic design, but these contributions have been mainly variations of basic European principles. Nor do I mean to deny the fact that an American designer such as Morris Benton, in redesigning such typefaces as Garamond and Bodoni, has done significant work. In this connection, however, it is my understanding that while the redesign of typefaces or the creation of new typefaces is vitally important, the typeface is only one ingredient in the overall design complex. It provides only the what and not the how. Furthermore, it is somewhat ironic to note the very generous use of European typefaces in the New American Typography. How many printed pieces use Venus, Standard, or Didot, not to mention the classical designs – Garamond, Caslon, Baskerville, Bodoni, Bembo – all of European origin?

It is difficult for me to think of any single book on modern American typography that would, for example, equal the Swiss publication *Typographische Monatsblatter,* let alone such classics as Tschichold's *Die Neue Typografie, Typographishe Gestaltung,* or even his later, more conventional *Designing Books.* In 1929 Douglas C. McMurtrie wrote *Modern Typography and Layout,* a book which contained some excellent illustrative material as well as some scholarly text. The makeup of this book, however, was in the modernistic style—a rather questionable example of typography, American or otherwise.

No fair-minded person, American or European, can deny the influence of the American designers Goudy, DeVinne, Bruce Rogers, and Dwiggins on both American and European typography. However, when we compare the enormous impact on modern typography of just one European designer—Jan Tschichold[1]—there is little doubt that the influence of the aforementioned designers has been far more limited.

1. This is still true today, even though Tschichold later switched to traditional typography.

Before we are able to evaluate the New American Typography, we must necessarily place it in its historical context—a rather difficult undertaking for designers, people engaged in doing rather than philosophizing. I believe that at the present time we are too close to the trees to evaluate the situation. No doubt in time we can hope to produce a more indigenous kind of typography, one which satisfies our basic needs through original formal solutions, rather than one which is obsessed with a style. I am afraid that at the present time it is impossible for me to answer the question, "What is this new form?"

Good typography, American or otherwise, is not a question of nationality but of sensitivity to form and purpose. In the twenties, when Tschichold wrote his revolutionary book on modern typography, he did not call it German or Swiss or French, he called it simply—*Die Neue Typografie.*

Twenty-five years have passed since the foregoing was written. If there is a typography uniquely American, it seems to be largely nostalgic, with the revival of such undistinguished typefaces as Bookman—chosen, I suppose, because it is judged to be more legible, more earthy, or less "designy." Spencerian flourishes and Victorian dingbats are also high on the agenda. Others, attempting to update the New Typography, seem infatuated with kitsch and concerned more with novelty than with form, with results that are merely bizarre. This is equally true of much of today's architecture.

It is my belief that only one style, based on aesthetic and practical principles and ideologically different from the classical past, has endured through these years. It has been variously described as the new typography or modern typography, and most often identified with the Swiss. As Cubism is to modern painting, the so-called Swiss style is to modern typography and design. The term Swiss is used not to designate a geographical region, but to indicate a genre —a kind of design international in origin, influence, and practice. It interprets visual space differently from its predecessors and is distinctly separated from traditional typography by asymmetric page arrangements, carefully chosen typefaces (usually sans serif), and strict avoidance of superfluities. Though not precise, the term Swiss seems appropriate since the Swiss have been the most methodical and consistent practitioners of this art. However, International Style would be a more accurate designation.

*Jacket design,
Wittenborn, Schultz, Inc.,
1951*

DADA

Poster,
U.S. Department of the Interior,
1974

Type design,
Westinghouse Electric Corporation,
1961

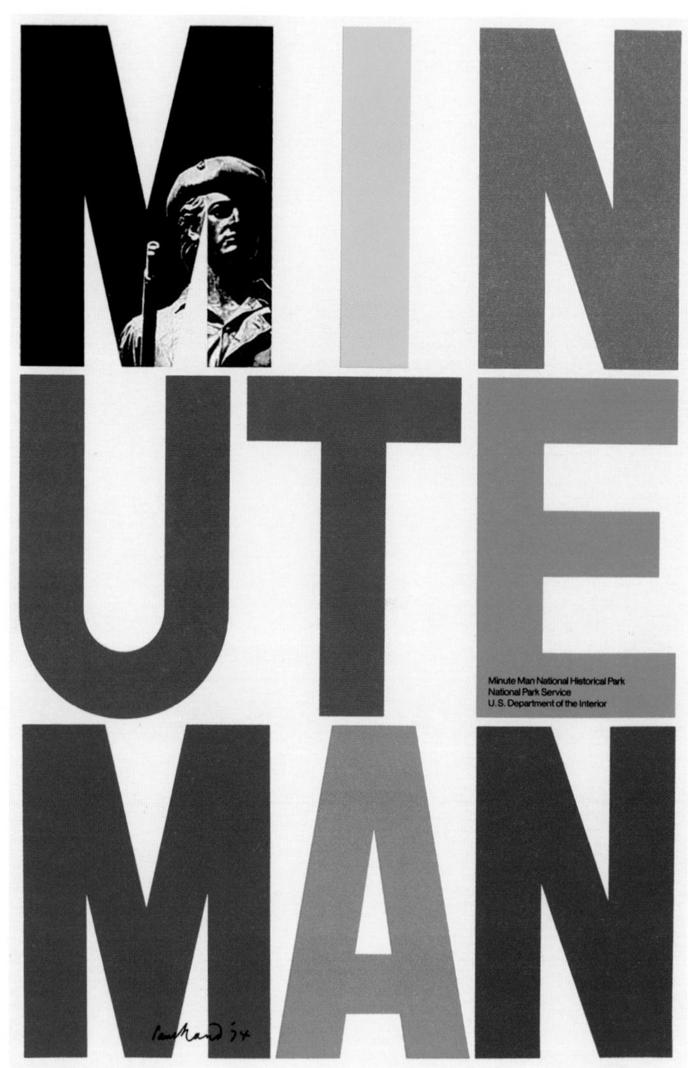

abcdef
mnop
vwxy
CDEFG
MNO
UVWXY
1234567890$¢!?.,

Jacket design,
Albert Bonnier,
1950

Annual Report,
Westinghouse Electric Corporation,
1974

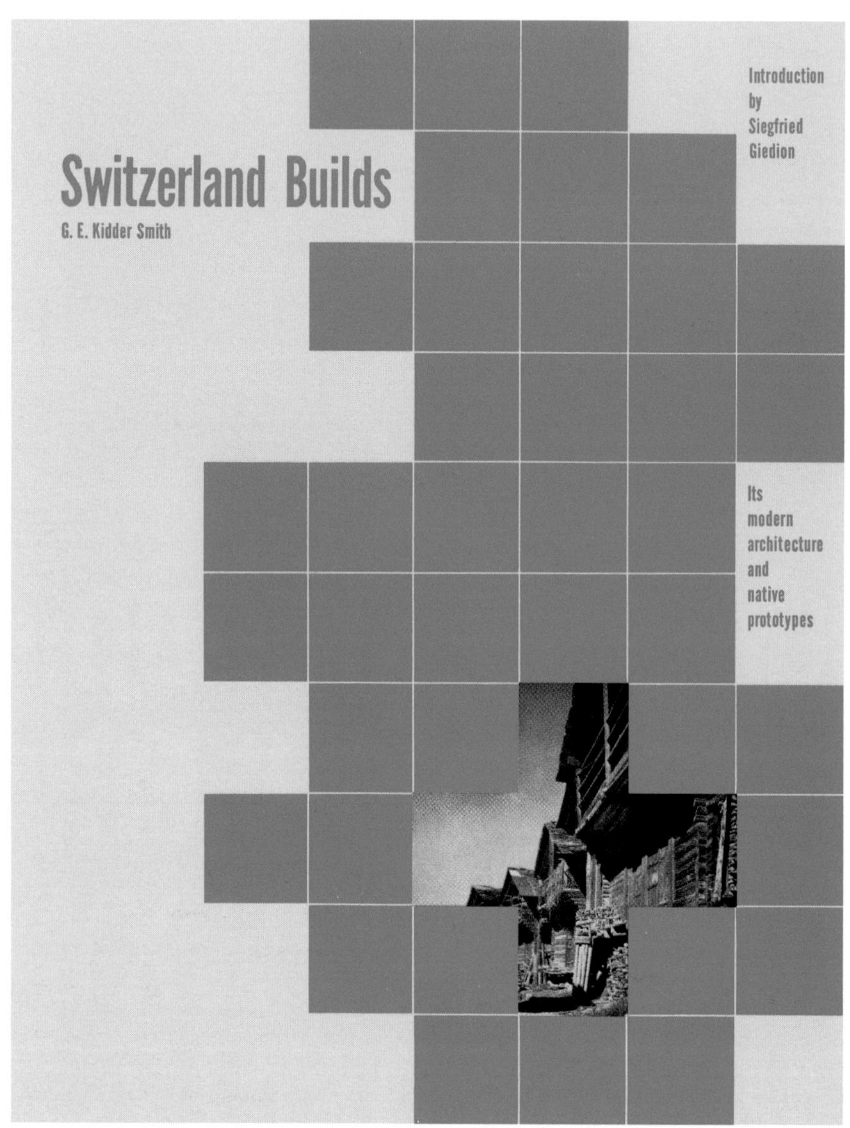

Switzerland Builds
G. E. Kidder Smith
Introduction
by
Siegfried
Giedion
Its
modern
architecture
and
native
prototypes

1974
Westinghouse Annual Report

Design and the Play Instinct

"I demand of art," says Le Corbusier, "the role of the challenger...of play and interplay, play being the very manifestation of the spirit."[1]

The absence in art of a well-formulated and systematized body of literature makes the problem of teaching a perplexing one. The subject is further complicated by the elusive and personal nature of art. Granted that a student's ultimate success will depend largely on his natural talents, the problem still remains how best to arouse his curiosity, hold his attention, and engage his creative faculties.

Through trial and error, I have found that the solution to this enigma rests, to a large extent, on two factors: the kind of problem chosen for study, and the way it is posed. I believe that if undue emphasis is placed on freedom and self-expression in the statement of a problem, the result is apt to be an indifferent student and a meaningless solution. Conversely, a problem with defined limits, with an implied or stated discipline (system of rules) that in turn is conducive to the instinct of play, will most likely yield an interested student and, very often, a meaningful and novel solution.

Two powerful instincts exist in all human beings which can be used in teaching, says Gilbert Highet: one is the love of play. "The best Renaissance teachers, instead of beating their pupils, spurred them on by a number of appeals to the play principle. They made games out of the chore of learning difficult subjects—Montaigne's father, for instance, started him in Greek by writing the letters and the easiest words on playing cards and inventing a game to play with them."[2]

Depending on the nature of the problem, some or all of the psychological and intellectual factors implicit in game-playing are equally implicit in successful problem-solving:

motivation	skill	excitement
competition	observation	enjoyment
challenge	analysis	discovery
stimulus	perception	reward
goal	judgment	fulfillment
promise	improvisation	
anticipation	coordination	
interest	timing	
curiosity	concentration	
	abstraction	
	discretion	
	discrimination	
	economy	
	patience	
	restraint	
	exploitation	

Without the basic rules or disciplines, however, there is no motivation, test of skill, or ultimate reward—in short, no game. The rules are the means to the end, the conditions the player must understand thoroughly and work with in order to participate. For the student, the limits of a well-stated problem operate in much the same way. "Limited means," says Braque, "beget new forms, invite creation, make the style. Progress in art does not lie in extending its limits, but in knowing them better."[3]

Unfortunately, in some of our schools little attempt is made to guide the student's thinking in a logical progression from basic design to applied design. We are all familiar with the so-called practical problems formulated by a teacher in an attempt to duplicate the conditions of industry—the atmosphere of the advertising agency, for example. Such problems are frequently stated in the broadest terms with emphasis, if any, on style and technique in advertising, rather than on interpreting advertising in terms of visual design principles.

1 Le Corbusier, *The Modulor* (Cambridge, MA, 1954), 220.

2 Gilbert Highet, *The Art of Teaching* (New York, 1950), 194.

3 *Cahier de Georges Braque* (Paris, 1947), 33.

Without specific formal limitations and without the challenge of play, both teacher and student cannot help but be bored. The product may take the form of a superficial (but sometimes "professional looking") literal translation of the problem, or of a meaningless abstract pattern or shape, which, incidentally, may be justified with enthusiasm but often with specious reasoning.

Similarly, there are badly stated problems in basic design that stress pure aesthetics and free expression without any restraints or practical goals. Such a problem may be posed in this fashion: arrange a group of geometric shapes in any manner you see fit, using any number of colors, to make a pleasing pattern. The results of such vagaries are sometimes pretty, but mostly meaningless or monotonous. The student has the illusion of creating great art in an atmosphere of freedom, when in fact he is handicapped by the absence of certain disciplines which would evoke ideas and make playing with those ideas possible, work absorbing, and results interesting.

The basic design problem, properly stated, is an effective vehicle for teaching the possibilities of relationships: harmony, order, proportion, number, measure, rhythm, symmetry, contrast, color, texture, space. It is an equally effective means for exploring the use of unorthodox materials and for learning to work within specific limitations.

To insure that theoretical study does not end in a vacuum, practical applications of the basic principles gleaned from this exercise should be undertaken at the proper time (they may involve typography, photography, page layout, displays, or symbols).

The student learns to conceptualize, to associate, to make analogies; to see a sphere, for example, transformed into an orange, or a button into a letter, or a group of letters into a broad picture. "The pupils," says Alfred North Whitehead, "have got to be made to feel they are studying something, and are not merely executing intellectual minuets."[4]

If possible, teaching should alternate between theoretical and practical problems, and between problems with tightly stated "rules" imposed by the teacher and problems with rules implied by the problem itself. But this can happen only after the student has been taught basic disciplines and their application. He then is able to invent his own system for "playing the game." "A mind so disciplined should be both more abstract and more concrete. It has been trained in the comprehension of abstract thought and in the analysis of facts."[5]

There are many ways in which the play principle serves as a basis for serious problem-solving, some of which are discussed here. These examples indicate, I believe, the nature of certain disciplines and may suggest the kinds of problems that will be useful to the student as well as to the teacher of design.

Alfred North Whitehead, *The Aims of Education* (New York, 1949), 21.

Ibid, 24.

The Romanesque church Badia de Fiesole exhibits surprising playfulness on every inch of its facade. (c. 850)

Crossword Puzzle

The crossword puzzle is a variation on the acrostic, a word game that has been around since Roman times. There have been many reasons given for the popularity of the game. It fulfills the human urge to solve the unknown; it is orderly; it represents, according to the puzzle editor of the *New York Times,* "a mental stimulation... and exercise in spelling and vocabulary-building."[6] But the play in such a game is limited to finding the exact word to fit a specific number of squares in a vertical and horizontal pattern. It allows for little imagination and no invention or aesthetic judgment, qualities to be found in abundance, for example, in the simple children's game, the Tangram.

6. *The New York Times Magazine,* December 15, 1963.

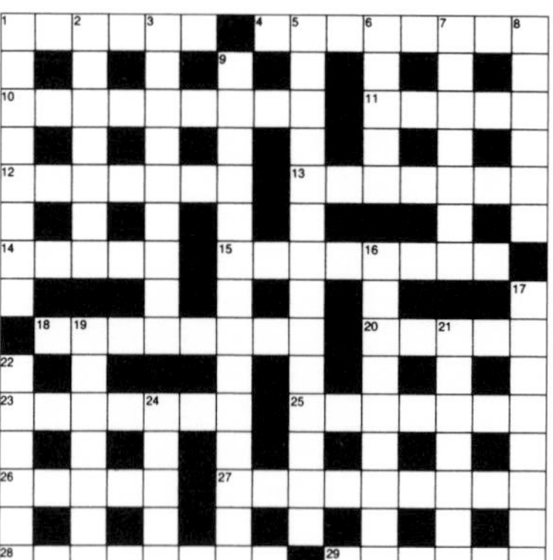

The Tangram

The Tangram is an ingenious little Chinese toy in which a square is divided into a special configuration. It consists of seven pieces, called *tans* : five triangles, one square, and one rhombus. The rules are quite simple : rearrange to make any kind of figure or pattern.

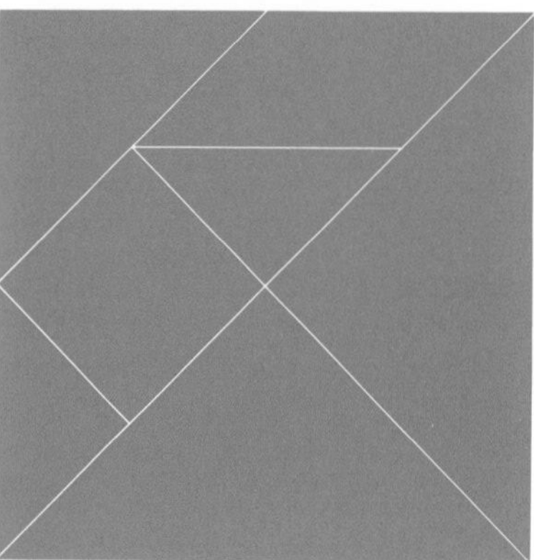

Here is one possibility. Many design problems can be posed with this game in mind; the main principle to be learned is that of economy of means—making the most of the least. Further, the game helps to sharpen the powers of observation through the discovery of resemblances between geometric and natural forms. It helps the student to abstract: to see a triangle, for example, as a face, a tree, an eye, or a nose, depending on the context in which the pieces are arranged. Such observation is essential in the study of visual symbols.

Hokusai's Drawing

This drawing is reproduced from the first volume of Hokusai's *Rapid Lessons in Abbreviated Drawing* (Riakougwa Hayashinan, 1812). In the book Hokusai shows how he uses geometric shapes as a guide in drawing certain birds. This exercise may be compared to the Tangram in that both use geometric means. The Tangram, however, uses geometry as an end in itself—to indicate or symbolize natural forms—whereas Hokusai uses it as a clue or guide to illustrating them. In the artist's own words, his system "concerns the manner of making designs with the aid of a ruler or compass, and those who work in this manner will understand the proportion of things."

Chinese Characters

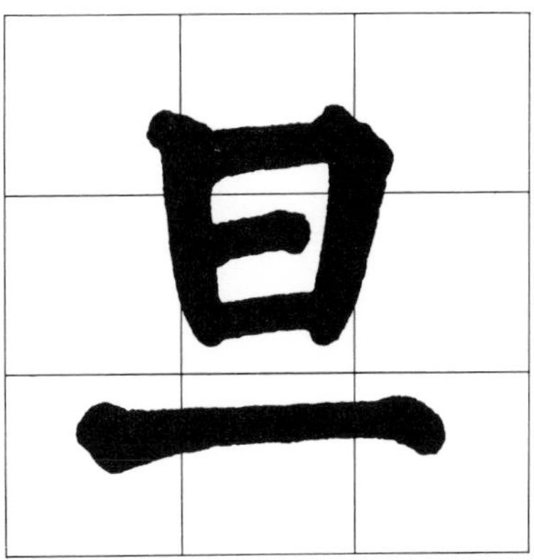

This character for the word *tan* (sunrise) is designed within an imaginary grid. Geometry functions here in a manner similar to the illustration above, namely as a guide to filling the space correctly, but not to producing a geometric pattern.

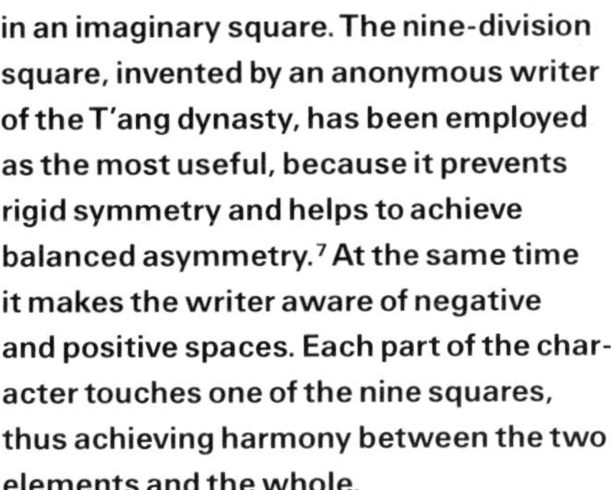

The Chinese character is always written in an imaginary square. The nine-division square, invented by an anonymous writer of the T'ang dynasty, has been employed as the most useful, because it prevents rigid symmetry and helps to achieve balanced asymmetry.[7] At the same time it makes the writer aware of negative and positive spaces. Each part of the character touches one of the nine squares, thus achieving harmony between the two elements and the whole.

Chiang Yee, *Chinese Calligraphy* (London, 1938), 167.

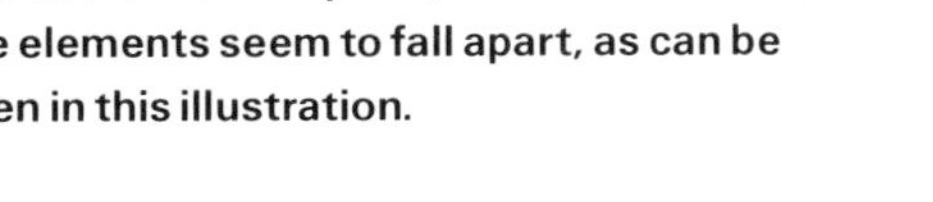

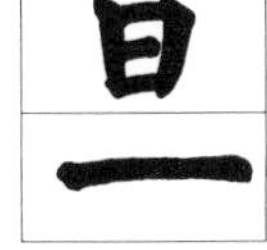

In a two-division square, on the other hand, the elements seem to fall apart, as can be seen in this illustration.

Within this rather simple discipline the calligrapher is able to play with space, filling it as he feels would be most appropriate. The composition of Chinese characters, says Chiang Yee, "is not governed by inviolable laws... however, there are general principles which cannot be ignored with impunity."[8]

Ibid., 166.

The Modulor

The Modulor is a system based on a mathematical key. Taking account of the human scale, it is a method of achieving harmony and order in a given work.

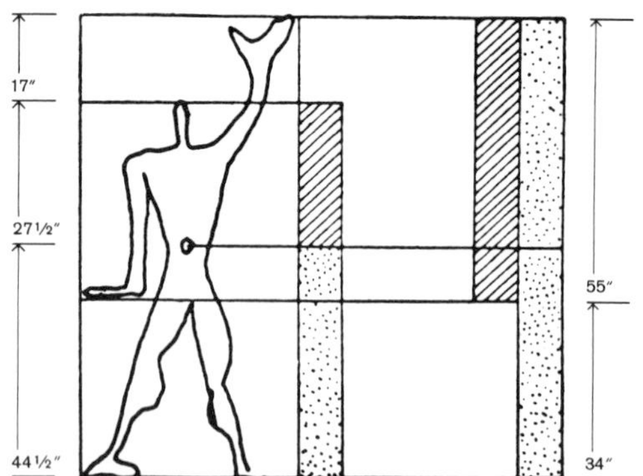

In his book, *The Modulor,* Le Corbusier describes his invention as "a measuring tool *[the proportions]* based on the human body *[six-foot man]* and on mathematics *[the golden section].* A man-with-arm-upraised provides, at the determining points of his occupation of space—foot, solar plexus, head, tips of fingers of the upraised arm—three intervals which give rise to a series of golden sections, called the Fibonacci series."[9] [1, 1, 2, 3, 5, 8, 13, etc.]

9. Le Corbusier, *The Modulor,* 55.

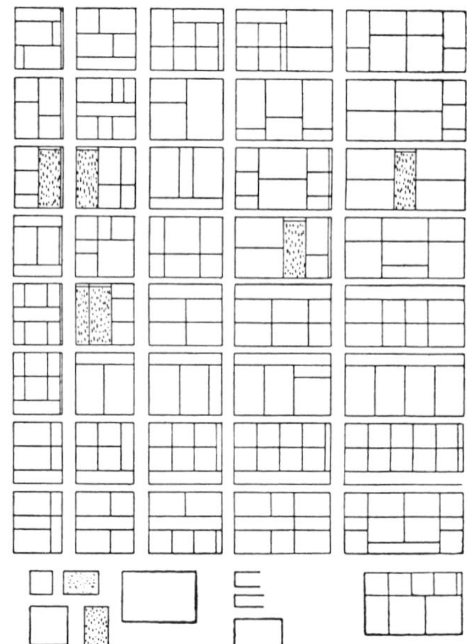

The Modulor is a discipline which offers endless variations and opportunities for play. Le Corbusier's awareness of these potentialities is evident from the numerous references to games and play in his book, such as "All this work on proportioning and measures is the outcome of a passion, disinterested and detached, an exercise, a *game.*" He goes on to say, "for if you want to *play modulor* . . ."[10]

10. Ibid., 80, 101.

In comparison to most so called systems of proportion, the Modulor is perhaps the least confining. The variations, as will be seen from this illustration, are practically inexhaustible (and this example utilizes only a very limited number of possibilities). This drawing is one of a limitless number of so-called Panel Exercises, played for pleasure or for some special application in order to discover a most satisfactory or beautiful configuration. If, however, the system should present any difficulties which happen to run counter to one's intuitive judgment, Le Corbusier himself provides the answer: "I still reserve the right at any time to doubt the solutions furnished by the Modulor, keeping intact my freedom which must depend solely on my feelings rather than on my reason."[11]

11. Ibid., 63.

The Grid System

Like the architect's plan, the grid system employed by the graphic designer provides for an orderly and harmonious distribution of miscellaneous graphic material. It is a system of proportions based on a module, the standard of which is derived from the material itself. It is a discipline imposed by the designer.

Unlike the Modulor, it is not a fixed system based on a specific concept of proportion, but one which must be custom-made for each problem. Creating the grid calls for the ability to classify and organize a variety of material with sufficient foresight to allow for flexibility in handling content that may, for one reason or another, be altered. The grid must define the areas of operation and provide for different techniques, pictures, text, space between text and pictures, columns of text, page numbers, picture captions, headings, and other miscellaneous items.

Here is the grid designed for this book. Devising such a grid involves two creative acts: developing the pattern that is suitable for the given material and arranging this material within the pattern.
In a sense, the creative ability required for the former is no less than that for the latter, because the making of the grid necessitates analyzing simultaneously all the elements involved. But once it has evolved, the designer is free to play to his heart's content: with pictures, type, paper, ink, and color, and with texture, scale, size, and contrast.

The grid, then, is the discipline that frees one from the time-consuming burden of making certain decisions (dimensions, proportions) without which fruitful and creative work is extremely difficult. One can move directly to those aspects of the problem in which individual expression, novel ideas, and freedom of choice are essential.

The grid system has as many detractors as it has adherents. Its detractors generally misunderstand its use or its potential – and that it is merely a tool. It has been condemned as stifling, rigid, and cold. But this confuses the product with the process. The grid does not automatically insure an exciting solution. The designer must still exercise all the experience at his command: discretion, timing, and a sense of drama and sequence. In brief, the intelligent designer will recognize that the grid can help him achieve harmony and order, but also that it may be abandoned when and if necessary.
To function successfully, the grid system, like all workable systems, must be interpreted as freely as necessary. It is this very freedom which adds richness and a note of surprise to what might otherwise be potentially lifeless.

Masons' Marks

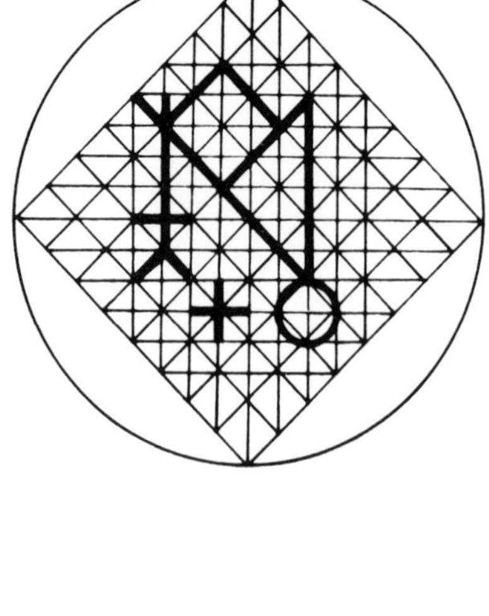

We find other variations of the geometric plan in Japanese architecture, modern painting, and Byzantine masons' marks, such as the seal at right. This seal "employs a mathematical key as its design basis. The thick lines represent the mark, the thin lines represent the ground lattice which allows an infinite number of combinations."[12] The geometric scheme is the discipline in which the designer works. Designs stemming from such a scheme are limited only by his imagination.

12. Matila Ghyka, *The Geometry of Art and Life* (New York, 1946), 120.

Tatami (floor mats)

The system employed by Japanese architects in designing their traditional houses both determines the size of various rooms in the house, as well as floors, walls, furniture, and creates the style and appearance of the house.

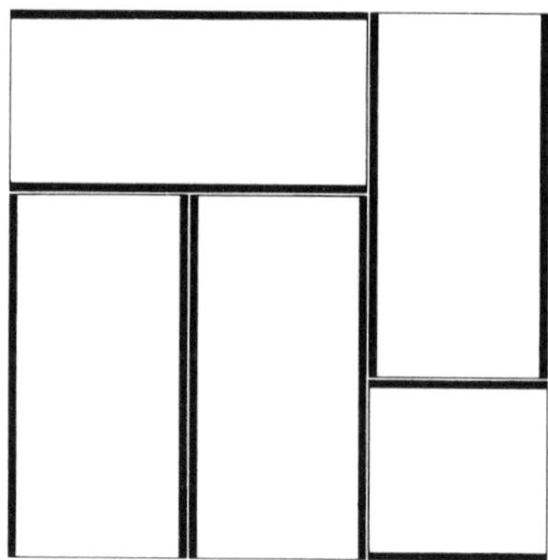

The Tatami, a straw mat approximately 3 by 6 feet and 2 inches thick, is the module or standard from which the plan of the house grows. Edward S. Morse, in his book *Japanese Homes,* describes the mat system as follows: "The architect invariably plans his rooms to accommodate a certain number of mats; and since these mats have a definite size, any indication on the plan of the number of mats a room is to contain gives at once its dimensions also. The mats are laid in the following numbers: two, three, four-and-one-half, six, eight, ten, twelve, fourteen, sixteen, and so on."[13] This illustration shows the plan of a four-and-one-half-mat room. Once the outer dimensions of the house are determined, the mats, together with the Japanese system of sliding doors, give complete flexibility in the arrangement and number of rooms. A perfect example of form and function, of discipline and play.

13. Edward S. Morse, *Japanese Homes* (Boston, 1885), 122.

Albers

Much of the painting of Josef Albers is based on the geometric pattern we see here. The pattern is not used, however, in the same manner as the masons' lattice. Here the pattern is the painting itself. It represents a strict, immutable arrangement (theme) in which the artist, by juxtaposing colors (variations), plays the fascinating game of deceiving the eye. The squares as we see them here appear to recede into the picture plane. However, by skillful manipulation of colors, the painting flattens out and is thus seen as a two-dimensional picture.

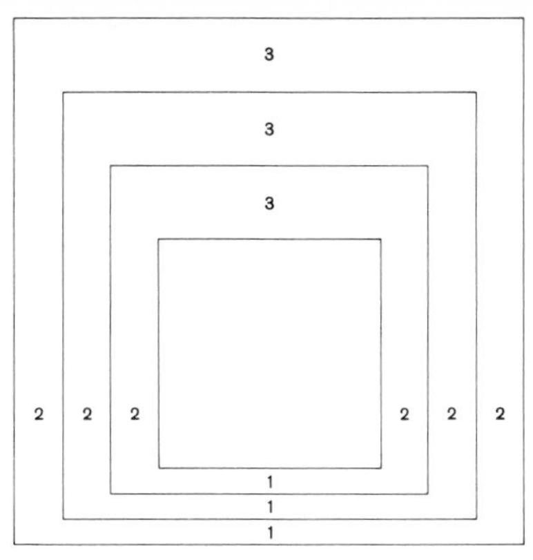

The many variations based on this and similar designs attest to the fascination Albers finds in the interplay of a great variety of color schemes and an extremely limited geometric format.

Cubist Collages

Similarly the early Cubist collages, in which cut paper played an important part, are products of strict rules, limited materials: newspaper mounted on a surface, with the addition of a few charcoal or pencil lines, usually in black and white; sometimes tan or brown or similarly muted colors were used. These elements were juggled until they satisfied the artist's eye. The playfulness and humor in the production of some of these compositions in no way detracts from the end result of a serious work of art. (Painting shown is Braque's *Clarinet*, private collection, New York)

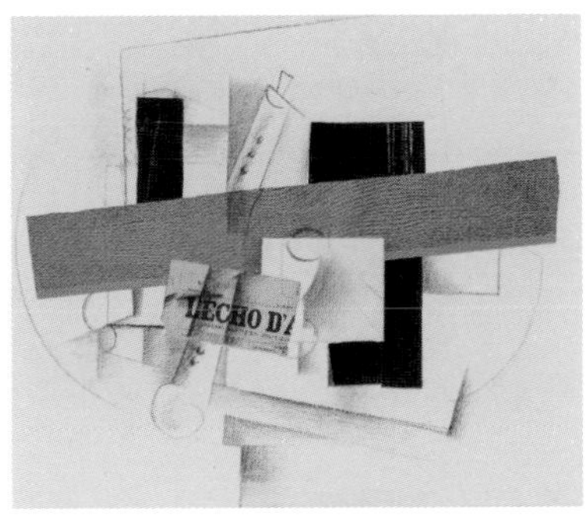

Matisse

It is inconceivable to consider Matisse's cut paper compositions without, in some way, linking them to the play element—the joy of working with simple colors and the fun of "cutting paper dolls." The greatest satisfaction, perhaps, is derived from creating a work of art with ordinary scissors and some colored paper—with so simple means, such satisfying ends.

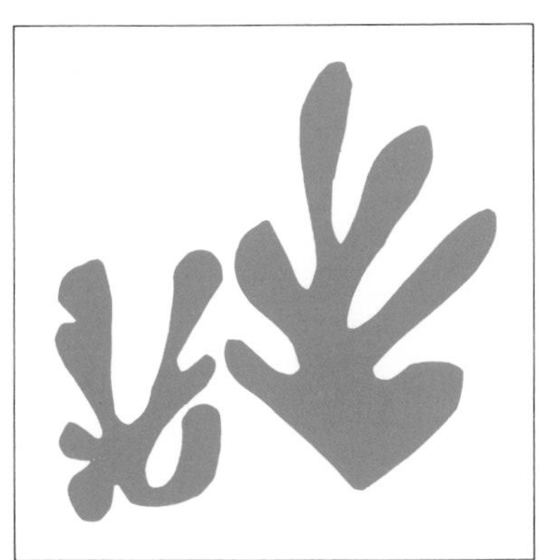

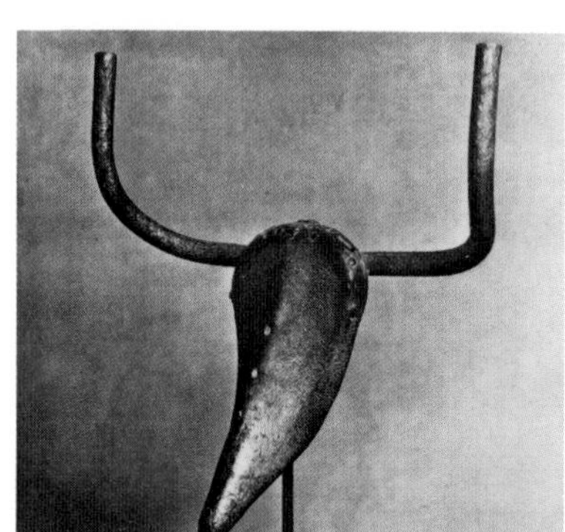

Picasso

One cannot underestimate the importance of restraint and playfulness in almost any phase of Picasso's work. Here, for example, one sees a straightforward use of the brush and a single color. The drawing of the child's face, the ornament, and the lettering are all one. Lettering is not used as a complement to the drawing, but as an integral part of it. It serves as both a garland and a verbal image – a visual pun. What emerges is itself a kind of game, revealing the ingenuity and playfulness of the artist, his ability to deal with problems in the simplest, most direct, and most meaningful manner.

Similarly, this ability to do much with little – to find a bull's head in a bicycle seat and handlebars – is another aspect of Picasso's wizardry, his humor, his childlike spontaneity, his skill as a punster, and his ability to improvise and invent with limited, often surprising means.

Mu Ch'i

This monochrome on the right, *Persimmons,* by Mu Ch'i, a thirteenth century Zen priest and painter, is a splendid example of a painting in which the artist plays with contrasts (the male and female principles in Chinese and Japanese painting): rough and smooth, empty and full, one and many, line and mass, black and white, tint and shade, up and down. It is a study in the metamorphosis of a fruit, as well as of a painting. (The artist, incidentally, never used any color but black.)

The reader may find a parallel, at least in spirit, between this painting and the preceding one by Picasso. Both employ a single color, both exploit this limitation to achieve as much variety as possible, and both undoubtedly were painted very rapidly, a condition often conducive to utmost simplification and improvisation.

The Photogram

The idea of the photogram or camera-less photography goes back as far as the 19th century with Fox Talbot's photogenic drawings. In our time the pioneers of photography without the use of a camera were Christian Schad, Man Ray, Moholy-Nagy, and Kurt Schwitters. Among the first to apply this technique in advertising was the constructivist El Lissitzky. Later, Picasso experimented with the photogram. In advertising, the photogram has yet to be fully exploited.

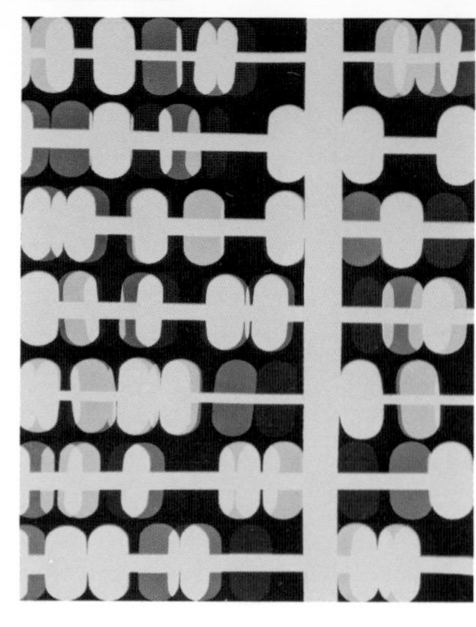

Although the effectiveness of the photogram depends chiefly on straightforward mechanical methods (light on sensitized paper), it offers the designer ample opportunity for aesthetic, manual control. In a sense, it is not a picture of the object but the object itself; and, as in stroboscopic photography, it makes picturization of continuous movement possible as in this photogram of an abacus, at right, by the author. (See also page 209.) Although some of its effects may be approximated with pen, brush, or scissors, the quality inherent in the subtle light modulations can be achieved, perhaps, only by means of the photogram.

Piet Zwart

The *de Stijl* movement, founded in 1917, had a profound influence on painting, architecture, and typography. Piet Zwart, the designer responsible for this advertisement for the Dutch firm Nederlansche Kabelfabriek, was associated with this group.

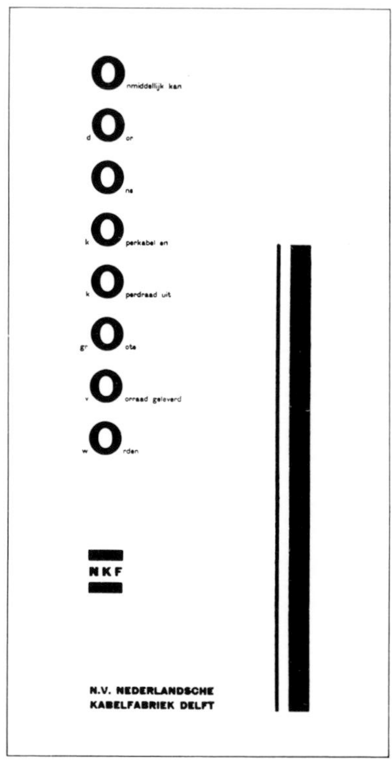

The disciplines which *de Stijl* encouraged are evident in this Zwart design: functional use of material and meaningful form, and the restrained use of color (black and/or primary colors). From a few simple typographic elements and an ingenious play on the letter O, a humorous, yet significant design evolved. A picture is created by typographic means: a few type characters and type rules are so manipulated as to make a useful product, an advertisement. Many examples of this artist's work reveal the same playful approach and are worthy of serious study.

Japanese Craftsman

The earth colors of Africa, the ice of the polar regions, and the bamboo of Japan are among the many challenging materials with which artists and artisans create their idols, their utensils, and their houses—all natural limitations that provide their own built-in disciplines which, in turn, contribute to the creative solution.

Some years ago in Kyoto I was fortunate enough to witness a young Japanese craftsman make the chasen you see here. The chasen is a whisk used in the tea ceremony and is cut from a single piece of bamboo with a simple tool resembling a penknife. Both the material and manufacturing process (which took about one-half hour) are the quintessence of discipline, simplicity, and restraint. The invention of such an article could not possibly have been achieved by anyone lacking the ability to improvise and the patience to play with a specific material: to see the myriad possibilities and to discover the ideal form.

Black Black Black

Taboos and prejudices have long created limiting barriers to experimentation and to meaningful work in the arts. Here I should like to attack one particular prejudice – that against the color black.[1]

> *Vowels: black A, white E, red I,*
> *green U, blue O,*
> *Someday I shall name the birth*
> *from which you rise:*
> *A is a black corset and over it*
> *the flies*
> *Boil noisy where the cruel stench*
> *fumes slow . . .*[2]

In these lines the French poet Rimbaud uses the word black to describe and symbolize carnality, death, and decay. This traditional association of the color black with death and sin is long-standing and has led to the widespread conviction in both art and lay circles that black is depressing and sinister and therefore, if possible, must be avoided. As a result, the power and usefulness of black has been limited or misunderstood. During this century many individual artists, architects, and designers have rebelled against the conventional use and misuse of black. However, the prejudices against this color are still sufficiently strong to require a discussion of the properties of black and a vigorous defense of its many virtues.

In nature, black and its companion color white are dramatically juxtaposed in the contrast between day and night. The monotony of uninterrupted darkness or light would be intolerable. Black in the trunks of trees subtly sets off the brilliance of green or autumn-colored leaves. Throughout nature we find the equivalent of black and white in shadow and light – there are caves and canyons as well as fields and meadows. Man as a rule does the least violence to nature when he uses either natural materials, such as stone or wood, or black and white for the objects he places out of doors. Natural colors are integrated: white participates by reflecting environmental color, and black modestly provides a perfect background for the riotous colors around it. Certainly those people who observed with pleasure the old-fashioned black steam engine wind its way agreeably through green fields and forests have watched with a kind of horror the orange or blue streamliner that now streaks garishly across the countryside.

The decidedly ambivalent nature of black has been understood in daily use. In parts of the United States and in Europe black is by far the most popular color for pleasure vehicles, but it is also the color of the hearse. In clothes black is the color of tragedy, mourning. At the same time it is the color of elegance and of sensuous enjoyment, à la conventionally sexy black lingerie. Black is also linked with mystery, with the unknowable, and with seclusion, fear, and magic.

In some countries black or near-black has been employed extensively in architecture and interior design. The color pattern of the Japanese house is based on the contrasting use of dark and light materials. Dark wood often delineates the basic structure of the house and separates it aesthetically from the light-colored partition walls *(fusuma)* and floor mats *(tatami).*

For many centuries Chinese and Japanese painters have revered black as a color. In Japanese painting, black *(sumi)* is often the only color employed. The Japanese artist feels that "colors can cheat the eye but *sumi* never can; it proclaims the master and exposes the tyro."[3] One famous Japanese painter, Kubota, frequently expressed the wish that he might live long enough to be able to discard color altogether and use "*sumi* alone for any and all effects in paintings."[4]

[1] It should be noted that it is impossible to discuss black without implying white, grays, and dark umbers the greater part of the time.

[2] By permission of the translator, Muriel Ruckeyser. Sergei Eisenstein, *The Film Sense* (New York, 1942), 90.

[3] Henry P. Bowie, *On the Laws of Japanese Painting* (San Francisco, 1911), 39.

[4] Ibid., 43

b l a

c 

It is of course understood that, as with any color, the value of black depends upon the manner in which it is used. Black will be lugubrious or bright and elegant depending on its context and form. Despite the successful use of black in Japan and in modern buildings and interiors, many people still deny black categorically. A doctor writing on the use of color in interiors issues a grim warning against black: "This is the most dismal of all colors – it expresses all that is opposite to white."[5] Among these opposites he lists the grave, sin, and crime.

5 Edward Podolsky, *The Doctor Prescribes Colors*.

This type of blanket denunciation of a color completely ignores the relative nature of any color or form. Eisenstein, writing about film, says: "Even within the limitations of a color-range of black and white...one of these tones not only evades being given a single 'value' as an absolute image, but can even assume absolutely contradictory meanings, dependent only upon the general system of imagery that has been decided upon for the particular film."[6] He goes on to illustrate this important point by the reversal of the role of black in relation to white in two films, *Old and New* and *Alexander Nevsky*. In the former, black signified things reactionary, outdated, and criminal, while white denoted happiness, life, and progress; in *Alexander Nevsky* white was the color of cruelty, oppression, and death, and black, identified with the Russian warriors, represented heroism and patriotism. Eisenstein's response to the surprise and protest of the critics at this reversal of traditional symbolism is to cite *Moby Dick's* famous white whale – the reader will recall that the leprous, livid whiteness of this whale symbolized the world's monstrous and baffling evil.

6 Sergei Eisenstein, *The Film Sense* (New York, 1942), 151-52.

7 Daniel Henry Kahnweiler, *The Rise of Cubism* (New York, 1949), 11.

During the Middle Ages and the Renaissance, black (with some notable exceptions) was treated as a linear element or was associated with modeling and chiaroscuro. In *The Rise of Cubism* Kahnweiler says: "Since it was the mission of color to create the form as chiaroscuro, or light that had become perceivable, there was no possibility of rendering local color or color itself."[7] Although Kahnweiler is referring to color in general, this statement applies very forcibly to black. In the twentieth century the possibilities of rendering color as a thing in itself, and not primarily as a description of three-dimensionality or "objectivated light," have been rediscovered and exploited. Coincident with this trend, black has come into its own as a positive "plastic" value.

Mies van der Rohe

The accompanying illustration shows a building designed by Mies van der Rohe in which black is a crucial aesthetic factor. The structural members of this steel building are exposed and painted black. The effect of this is manifold: the structure is clearly defined, it is placed in dramatic contrast to the pale nonbearing brick walls, the bulk of its members is reduced (making them appear light and delicate), great elegance is achieved without the use of expensive materials or decoration, and the restraint and restfulness of black makes the building a welcome oasis in the chaotic heart of the city.

Arensberg collection.

A typographic example is the cover of this catalogue for the Arensberg Collection for the Art Institute of Chicago. This cover is composed of a series of contrasts, the most important of which is black and white. Together black and white act as complementary colors. Chevreul described them as such because when they are juxtaposed each becomes more vivid. This, he says, is due to the fact that the bright light reflected by the white area nullifies the reflected light from the black area. This makes the black seem blacker and the white more brilliant.

The tension between black and white in the cover is heightened by opposing a large area of black to a small area of white. The contrast theme is carried out further by the drastic variation in the size of the letters. The roughness of the edges of the large A emphasizes the sharpness of those of the smaller A's, and the extreme diagonals of the letters are counteracted by the right angles of the book itself. But the most dramatic element of contrast lies in the use of black and white. Black and white lend dignity and elegance to the book cover, yet the vigorous contrast between the two gives it a poster-like quality.

Thomas B. Stanley in *The Technique of Advertising Production* (New York, 1947) says: "While color has high attention value on short exposure, psychological tests indicate that the longer the time during which advertisements are examined, the more a black and white treatment tends to regain the attention lost at first glance to a color competitor."

Many advertisers and artists feel that an ad becomes more colorful in proportion to the amount of color used in it. This may or may not be true. Limited color combined with black and white, which provide a brilliant but neutral background, is often far more effective than the use of many colors. Furthermore, the tendency of black and white to brighten and enliven other colors often makes any color used seem more alive than when the color is used alone or in combination with other colors, as in this example.

It is impossible to define cold without contrasting it with heat. It is impossible to comprehend life if death is ignored. Black *is* the color of death, but by virtue of this same psychological fact it is also the color of life—it defines, contrasts, and enhances life, light, and color. It is through the artist's awareness of black as a polar element and consequently of its paradoxical nature that the color black can be appreciated and effectively used. And the artist must not forget that its neutrality makes black the common denominator of a multicolored world.

In 1860 Chevreul wrote: "I do not know whether the use of black for mourning prevents the use of it, in numberless cases, where it would produce most excellent effects."[8] This quotation is as pertinent today as it was in the nineteenth century. Most graphic artists still shy away from black. When they are confronted with no alternative other than black, as in newspaper advertising or typography, they often accept it grudgingly and make little effort to discover or develop its potentialities. However, the psychological and physical qualities of black which have been discussed so far in relation to architecture and painting are equally significant for the graphic arts. Here is an example of a photogram[9] for a cover design in which black plays a very significant role.

8. M. E. Chevreul, *The Laws of the Contrast of Color* (London, 1883), 54.

9. The photogram attained the status of a legitimate art form as a result of the pioneering work done by such people as Man Ray and Moholy-Nagy. Since then it has become increasingly popular in the graphic field.

Although this photogram is technically a light and shadow picture of an abacus, it is primarily a pattern of light and dark forms that seem to move horizontally across the surface. Because the photogram is an abstraction the plastic qualities of the object become more important than its literal ones.

One of the prime sources of the visual power of the photogram lies in its black, white, and gray tonality. The photogram portrays a world of light, shadow, and darkness peopled by mysterious suggestive forms. The ability of these forms to stimulate varied and imaginative associations in the mind of the spectator is weakened when the photogram is translated into color. A black and white photogram translated into one or more colors usually seems merely "colored" and evokes the unpleasant appearance of a retouched photograph.

Jacket design,
Wittenborn, Schultz, Inc.
1947

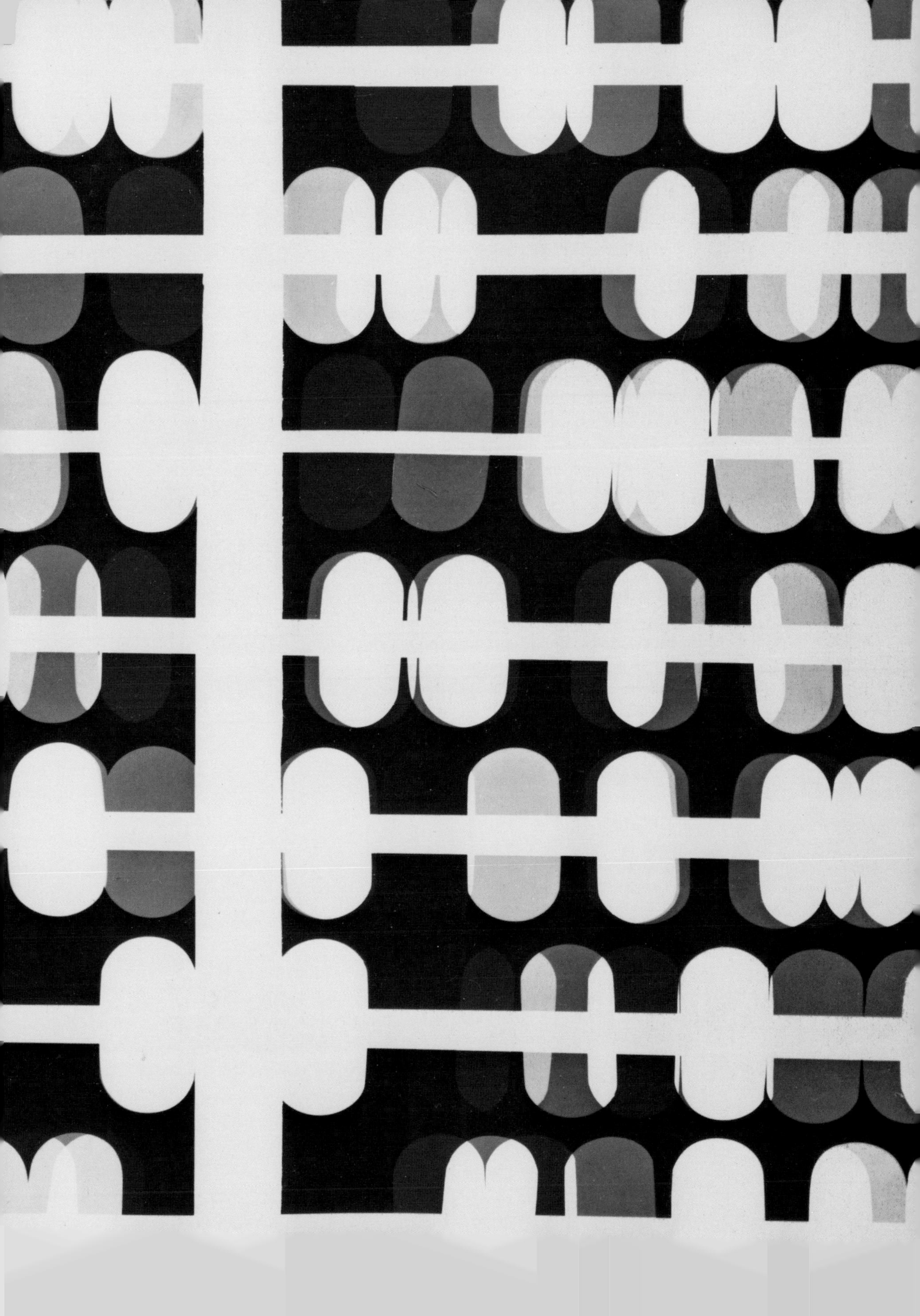

Arp

Arp, describing the painting reproduced here, says: "The black grows deeper and deeper, darker and darker before me. It menaces me like a black gullet. I can bear it no longer. It is monstrous. It is unfathomable.

As the thought comes to me to exorcise and transform this black with a white drawing, it has already become a surface. Now I have lost all fear, and begin to draw on the black surface. I draw and dance at once, twisting and winding, a winding, twining soft white flowery round. A round of snakes in a wreath... white shoots this way and that."[10]

10. Jean Arp, *On My Way* (New York, 1948), 82.

Picasso's *Guernica*

Picasso's *Guernica* (detail shown) is eloquent testimony of the expressive power of black and its natural companions gray and white. Although we do not know the intentions of the artist, we can venture a few statements about the more obvious effects achieved by the substitution of black, white, and gray for polychromatic colors. The absence of the expected pictorial colors in this mural dramatizes the impact of the work. Furthermore, the lack of color implies all colors and forces the spectator's imagination into activity by not telling him everything. The use of black, white, and gray is an understatement which makes possible and bearable the horror and violence of the imagery. At the same time, paradoxically, it emphasizes the brutally tragic imagery. It is probably beyond question that in this mural black and white play their ancient, symbolic roles. They are the raw unadulterated colors of the struggle between life and death.

Jean Arp, Vegetation, Oil on canvas, 1946. Private collection, Zurich.

In this magazine advertisement black functions as a foil for brilliant colors as well as a most dramatic contrast for the bright white bulbs. (Westinghouse, 1975)

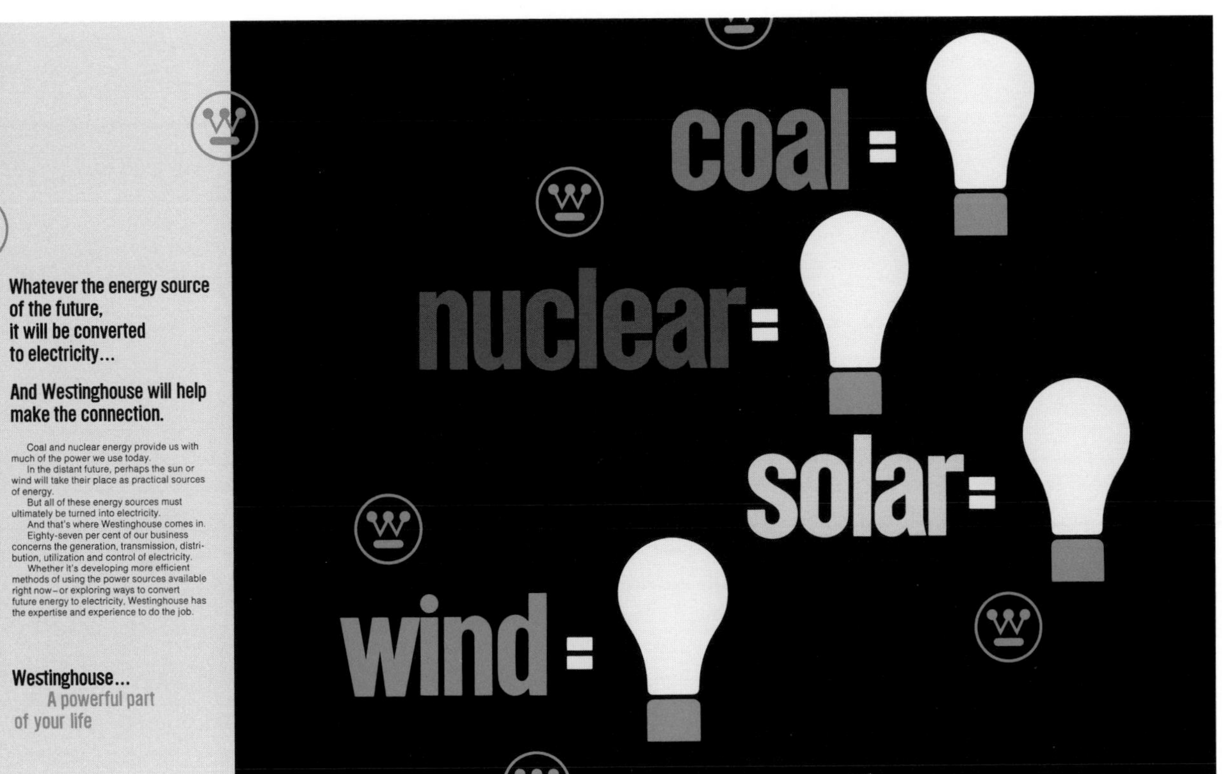

Whatever the energy source of the future, it will be converted to electricity...
And Westinghouse will help make the connection.
Coal and nuclear energy provide us with much of the power we use today.
In the distant future, perhaps the sun or wind will take their place as practical sources of energy.
But all of these energy sources must ultimately be turned into electricity.
And that's where Westinghouse comes in.
Eighty-seven per cent of our business concerns the generation, transmission, distribution, utilization and control of electricity.
Whether it's developing more efficient methods of using the power sources available right now–or exploring ways to convert future energy to electricity, Westinghouse has the expertise and experience to do the job.
Westinghouse...
A powerful part of your life
coal =
nuclear =
solar =
wind =

The Art of the Package: Tomorrow and Yesterday

"Art was born of man's need to leave his mark on Things."

– Rene Huyghe

"I'm not so concerned with the art or graphics of package design as I am with new developments in packaging technique – new materials, new construction and new applications." This statement was made some years ago by a specialist in package design. Today the tawdriness of most supermarket shelves bears witness to this lack of emphasis on decent design in our daily lives.

Technical advance in the field of packaging has been impressive indeed: the one-piece "flip-top," the push-button container, the shining array of new plastics with ingenious closures, the cleverly contrived shapes that stack, fit refrigerators or pockets, collapse, expand, and so forth. But does all this make a package? No. There is more to a package than convenience; it has to be looked at. How many flip-top cigarette packs or regular cigarette packs, for that matter, afford any pleasure to the eye? How consistently are we blinded by the dazzling display of vulgarity eagerly provided by most aerosol cans, cereal boxes, soaps, bread wrappers, etc.? Many, admittedly, are cleverly packaged. Technologically, scientifically, and hygienically packages of today are practical, but are they beautiful? Functionalism does not preclude beauty, but it certainly does not guarantee it either.

Indifference to aesthetic problems and the espousal of vulgarity probably derive mainly from the advertiser's single-minded preoccupation with having his product noticed and then quickly identified. In the frantic hope of "standing out," he tries to outshout, outcolor, and outglitter his competitor. He approves gaudy color schemes, oversized or misshapen lettering embellished with outlines, double or triple shadows, pseudo-Victorian decorations, and other exhibitionistic devices.

Good surface design is a complex matter. It does not automatically result from the fortuitous discovery of new materials, ingenious closures, or novel gimmicks, any more than it derives from blatant display. Surface design should in no way imply superficiality, for it often gives the designer the opportunity to enrich and personalize and articulate an otherwise bare and anonymous shape. Such a goal can be accomplished with a design as simple as a Chanel label or as complex as this Guinness label.

The obsession with functional shapes and new materials is a questionable limitation even for the conscientious designer blessed with a sensitive client. It tends to promote a misconception of simplicity, translating this admirable quality into bareness or rendering it self-conscious to the point of vapidity. This tendency is pronounced in many cigarette packs which have invaded the marketplace.

We often favor fancy, old fashioned designs for their charm and nostalgic appeal. What is the quality that makes a well-designed, simple, contemporary package design appealing? What is the quality that makes so many old traditional designs appealing? How does one capture these qualities without imitating them? Understanding their formal visual attributes is a way to begin.

Understanding means, among other things, that the designer must differentiate between the graphic possibilities of metal and plastic, glass and pottery, or paper and foil, flat and glossy, red and blue. Dignity, like understanding, is a general term, a principle of action. It does not mean that a product name should be small when a large one would be more effective or that ornament should or shouldn't be used. It means that a sense of dignity and the respect for work that accompanies it are indispensable guides to the designer in determining such formal problems of when, where, and how. If a designer treats his work with understanding, he will, for instance, recognize the anecdotal or associative aspects of pictorial symbols as well as the psychological and physiological effects of color. He will know that buyers have visual memories and are fond of the familiar. He will then be better able to decide in redesigning an old package which elements should be retained, discarded, altered, or refined. He will be aware of the nostalgic appeal of old cigar boxes, Pears Soap wrappers, the RCA Victor dog and will wonder about the wisdom of streamlining the White Rock girl or redesigning logos just because they've been around for a long time.

Although it is only possible to deal in generalities when it comes to a description of artistic principles, it is useful to show them in action. The following illustrations will demonstrate better than words some of the points I have tried to make.

The Chinese jardiniere *(Kang Hsi, 1662–1722), although not in the strictest sense a package, poses the same problems that the design of any cylindrical package does–namely, working on a curved surface. It is virtually impossible to imagine this vase without the bands of calligraphy which cover its entire surface, so in harmony with its form is the applied design. True, shape and proportion would remain unchanged, but the enriching exploitation of material, the emphasizing of contour, excitement of pattern, and the interest of the message (poem) would unhappily be lost.*

驩然交欣千載一會論說無疑翼乎如鴻毛遇順
風沛乎若巨魚縱大壑其得意如此則胡禁不止
曷令不行化溢四表橫被無窮遐夷貢獻萬祥必
臻是以聖主不遍窺望而視已明不殫傾耳而聽
已聰恩從祥風翱德與和氣遊太平之責塞優游
之望得遵游自然之勢恬淡無為之場休徵自至
壽考無疆雍容垂拱永永萬年何必偃仰屈伸若
彭祖呴噓呼吸如喬松眇然絕俗離世哉詩曰濟
濟多士文王以寧蓋信乎其以寧也

聖主得賢臣頌

Chanel packaging is perhaps a classic in its field. Each formal ingredient makes a contribution of itself and for the whole – the color and quality of the paper used, the trademark and how it is positioned as well as its size and weight, the black border complementing the circular trademark, the typeface (traditionally considered more suitable for Mack trucks), and finally the shape, size, and proportion of the boxes and bottles themselves. The combination of ingredients is indivisible and to remove any one would destroy the identity and beauty of the package. The Chanel design is an excellent study in visual contrasts.

Some time ago, in an exhibition of packaging at the Museum of Modern Art a bottle of Odol mouthwash was prominently displayed, but it could only be identified by those familiar with its unusual shape, since the label, ironically, was removed. This, I imagine, was because the bottle looked better without it. The actual label is rather bland, yet one can conceive of a label design which would not only serve its prime function – product identification – but also enhance the already beautiful form by enriching or emphasizing its shape.

At first glance it is difficult to ascertain why the package of tobacco pictured here is so attractive. Is it the ornament, color, type, paper, texture, or mere nostalgia? Looking closely we find it is a fine study in contrasts: plain brown paper, white label, ornamental border, and period typography. It is a soft package which contrasts with the brittle ornamentation of its surface design. The package suggests its contents and does so with grace and dignity. Even though some of the visual ingredients are not perfect, the ensemble is eminently satisfying. Similar qualities characterize the Garnier Elixir wood bottle.

The examples shown, both simple and complex, demonstrate that the package designer's problem is not essentially one of looking for new materials, but of understanding the importance of the artist's hand in relation to those materials, whether they be old or new. A good package of yesterday, today, or tomorrow expresses the respect of the artist for his materials in that he neither overwhelms them with meaningless or contrived ornament nor strips them of all interest and excitement out of a kind of Constructivist fetish. In a well-designed package the designer does not seek to exploit the consumer's visual memories and attachments by sentimental distortion but to express his objective appreciation of the fact that people do have strong affective reactions to "things."

With the exception of the Chanel packaging by Madame Chanel (c. 1925), the designers of the packages on these and previous pages are unknown. On the following pages some of the author's work in this and related fields is shown.

The Third Dimension

A graphic designer deals principally with printed matter—with two-dimensional space problems. Frequently, directly or indirectly, he ventures into the world of the three dimensional. Packaging must be dealt with as a two *and* three dimensional problem. The angles from which a bottle or package may be viewed are important considerations for the package designer. The problems of optical illusion and visual distortion are but a few considerations about which the designer must be aware.

Architecture, exterior or interior, may be interpreted as an overblown package seen from a certain point of view. The interiors of the IBM Product Centers comprise problems of two and three dimensions. The basic concept is essentially visual, not structural. The visual theme is based on the predominance of a single color, red. It could have been any appropriate color, but the idea of a single color is basic to the planned effect of the store interiors.

The color is applied to many different things, but not to the walls or ceilings. Carpeting, interior wall signs, and free-standing floor signs are all in red, with occasional white or gray accents. Typewriter stands, as in this photograph, are painted red. They are designed to disappear visually, to help focus attention on the products exhibited. Sign supports and table legs are painted red for the same reason: to make them disappear. White or offwhite walls and display fixtures are in dramatic contrast to the red carpeting which, incidentally, reflects a rosy glow on walls and ceilings.

The general effect of these shops, especially when viewed from the outside at night, is warm and welcoming. Incandescent down-lights were specified to provide the proper color balance, and to avoid harsh contrasts, and unpleasant color changes.

Further, to reinforce store identity, the scheme incorporates a special geometric device in the shape of a racetrack. This motif is not confined to two-dimensional items, such as the identification symbol, wall signs, and printed material, but is also used to determine the shape of table tops, display counters, and inclosed interior spaces of some of the shops.

The overall visual concept of the IBM Product Centers, including miscellaneous furniture displays, and graphics, was designed by the author in 1981.

Typing...
Error-Free
Typing...
Error-Free
Typing...
Portability Plus!
Two-Media Flexibility!
A Variety of Type Styles!
Try it!

IBM Wheelprinter Starter Pac
IBM Wheelprinter Starter Pac
IBM Wheelprinter Starter Pac
Wheelprinter Starter Pac
2 IBM Cartridge Printwheels II
18 IBM 9756 Ribbons
High Quality...

Package designs,
IBM Corporation,
1973-1984

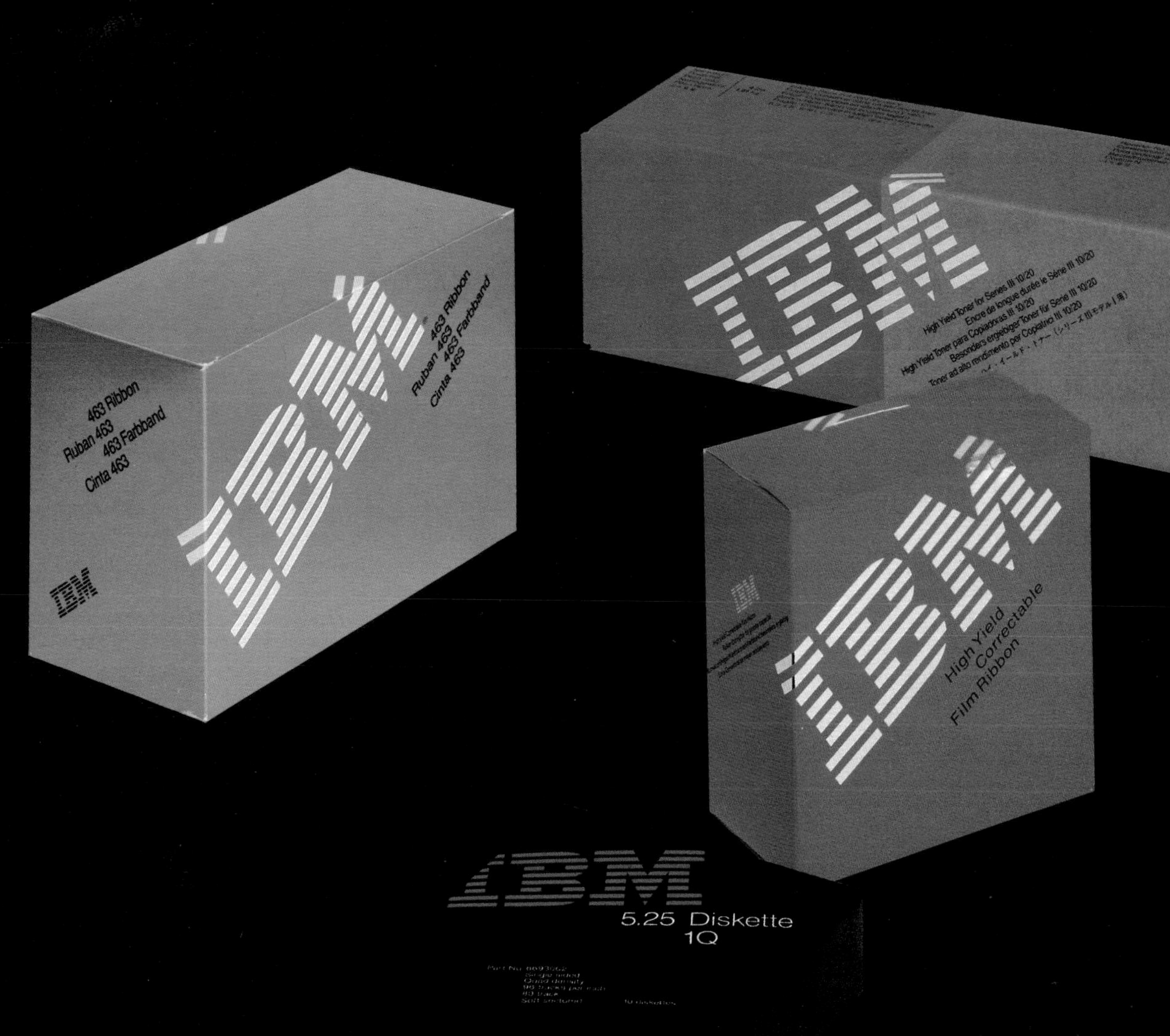

nutri-cola
NUTRI-COLA
nutri-cola
nutri-cola

Bottle design,
Nutri Cola Bottling Company,
1947

Package designs,
G.H.P. Cigar Company,
1953-1954

Package designs,
Cummins Engine Company, 1974,
Fleetguard, 1975

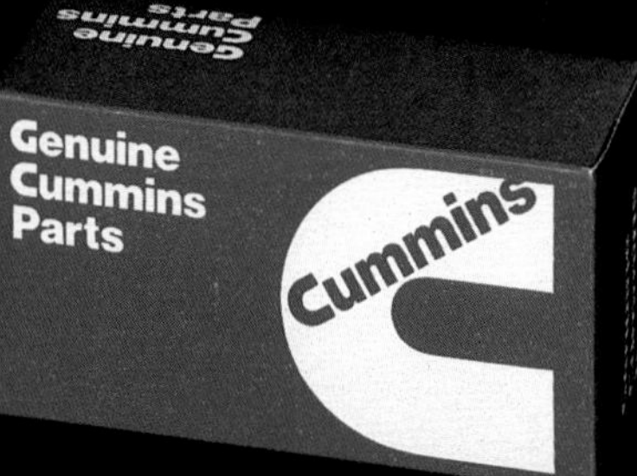

The Complexity of Color

Color theories of Goethe, Chevreul, Ostwald, Rood, or Munsell, among others, are not much help when facing a blank canvas. Color is objective; color is subjective. A color that is perfect in one instance is useless in another. Color is complexity personified. The use of color implies a knowledge, or at least an awareness, not only of the mechanics of color, but also of the formal, psychological, and cultural problems involved. Color cannot be separated from its physical environment without changing.

Like design problems, color is a matter of relationships:

materials
textures
finishes
light
shade
reflection

figure ground
contrasts
proportions
quantities
proximity
congruity
repetition

shape
content

How often have we seen the "perfect color" (in a room, a painting, a sky, a rug, a dress, a paint shop, or paper mill) without being aware of the implications of the surroundings in which this color resides – of the lighting, the architecture, the furniture, the hubbub, the silence, or our own state of mind?

Henri Matisse, *Jazz*, Editions Verve (Paris, 1947).

Matisse in his *Jazz*[1] puts the problem in another way. Following is a paraphrase describing the problem of painting a bouquet of flowers: Walking in his garden one day he picks a bunch of flowers with the idea of painting a bouquet. After arranging the bouquet to his own taste, he discovers that the charm in first perceiving these flowers is now lost. He attributes this to the reminiscences of long dead bouquets that have influenced the arrangement of this new bouquet. And he ends by quoting Renoir: "When I have arranged a bouquet for the purpose of painting it, I always turn to the side I did not plan."

"Le Bouquet. Dans une promenade au jardin je cueille fleur après fleur pour les masser dans le creux de mon bras l'une après l'autre au hasard de la cueillette. Je rentre à la maison avec l'idée de peindre ces fleurs. Après en avoir fait un arrangement à ma façon quelle déception: tout leur charme est perdu dans cet arrangement. Qu'est-il donc arrive? L'assemblage inconscient fait pendant la cueillette avec le goût qui m'a fait aller d'une fleur à l'autre est remplacé par un arrangement volontaire sorti de réminiscences de bouquets morts depuis longtemps, qui ont laissé dans mon souvenir leur charme d'alors dont j'ai chargé ce nouveau bouquet." Rénoir m'a dit: "Quand j'ai arrangé un bouquet pour le peindre, je m'arrète sur le côté que je n'avais pas prévu."

Coming quite casually on a scene like the one pictured on the following page, one is immediately taken by the stunning combination of brilliant colors and realizes how the neighboring scenery, earth, contrasting hues and textures, tints and shades cooperate to make this aesthetically appealing arrangement.

Word Pictures

Teaching art (design), perhaps more than other disciplines, involves a special kind of commitment from both teacher and student. Most complex is the task of formulating the problem. Ideally, an assignment should be so conceived as to be palatable, challenging, and absorbing, inviting curiosity and encouraging exploration. It should deal not only with formal but with manual skills. Following is a problem description which attempts to fulfill some of these varied and desirable goals.

Visual Semantics

Visual semantics deals with the use and manipulation of words (letters) to illustrate an idea, an action, or evoke some particular pictorial image. This involves the treatment and arrangement of letters in such a way as to make a word visually self-explanatory.

Problem

Develop three designs with the word "Léger." From the group of four specified colors (listed later) use only black for your first version, add a second color for the next, and use four for the last. Designs two and three should be seen as variations of the basic idea. Although not conceptually different, they should *look* different by virtue of the way in which the color is manipulated. Merely changing the background without some other meaningful alteration does not constitute an acceptable variation.

Visual analogies which most clearly illustrate meaning or spirit of a word should be sought; for example, the letter O could be the visual equivalent of the sun, a wheel, an eye. If additional elements are needed to reinforce your interpretations they should be simple, geometric shapes: circles, triangles, oblongs; also benday screens or typographical material such as rules, bullets, or mathematical signs.

Simple letters are preferred to fancy ones. Letters which imitate exotic alphabets or eccentric shapes should be avoided. Letters drawn accurately by means of ruler and compass are more suitable than freehand forms. (The reference here does not pertain to normally handwritten letters which possess their own peculiar characteristics.) The quality issuing from any process (facture), mechanical or otherwise, is a reflection of that particular process, and the visual effect (style) is intimately related to it. The more anonymous the letterforms (unencumbered by individual eccentricities or sentimental associations) the more meaningful. Originality is related more to the unexpected idea than to some flamboyant or peculiar technique. To defamiliarize the commonplace, to see it as if it were for the first time, is the artist's goal.

Fernand Léger

An important aspect of this problem is to discover the fundamental ideas and design principles governing the work of Fernand Léger, but not to mimic his work. Many of the working procedures and design processes, formal and otherwise, that concern all artists, are especially discernible in Léger's work. As subject matter he favored the commonplace, so as to minimize psychologically extraneous associations and to emphasize form. He translated subjects into objects. He saw the human figure as an inanimate object, not unlike a bottle or a guitar. The visual power of the machine, which he saw as a "tool of a social liberation" and a thing of beauty, was interpreted with great force, in its fixed and, particularly, in its moving state. He was obsessed by the idea of movement.

The means of achieving contrast and creating ambivalent space were deliberately sought and thoroughly explored. He usually treated background and foreground of his pictures with equal emphasis, in a lively, competitive relationship, or as a dialogue between abstraction and representation, between the real and the imaginary. He separated color from its form and studiously avoided the use of local color, thus calling attention both to color and to its object. Free color, free form, free association, and fresh visual combinations were devices he used to animate the two-dimensional picture plane and defamiliarize the commonplace.

Jennifer Kim,
Yale (Brissago, Switzerland),
1984

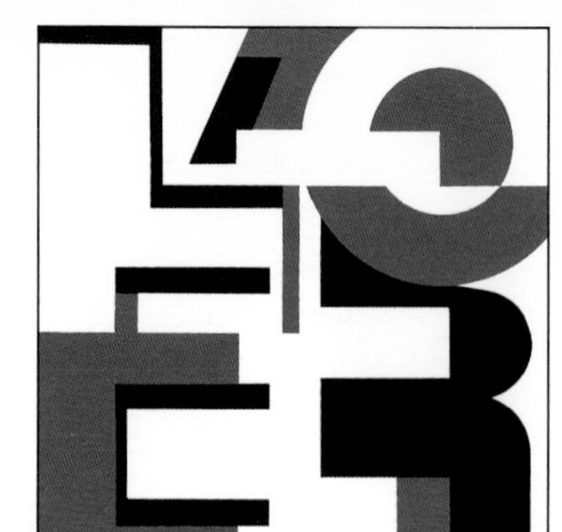

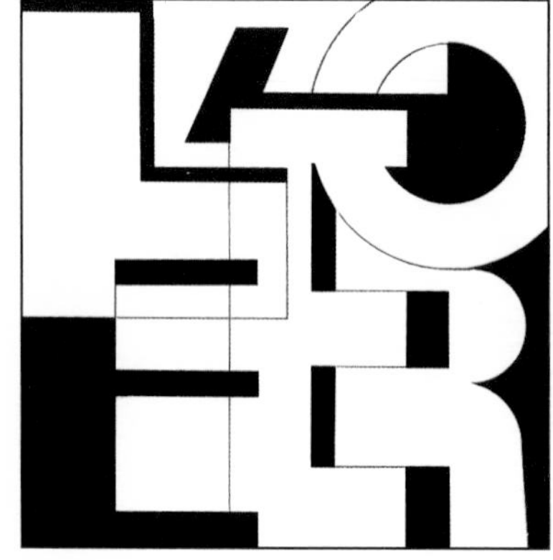

Contrast, simultaneity, repetition, and the elimination of conventional space illusion were uppermost in Léger's thoughts. Following are some of the pictorial means he used to realize his ideas:

Overlapping (space illusion)
Shifting (movement)
Enlarging (closeup, microscopic view)
Exaggerating (color, shape)
Neutralizing (objects, people)
Floating (against gravity)
Distorting (odd scale)
Cutting (cropping)
Fragmenting (part for whole)
Dividing (negative-positive)
Framing (picture within a picture)
Rearranging (nonconventional)
Coordinating (harmonizing)
Repeating (patterns)
Grouping (crowding, simultaneity)
Isolating (scattering)

Colors:
Venetian red, raw umber, gray blue, deep gray.

Apart from any psychological and symbolic associations, color is largely a problem of quantitative relationships. Color values change optically in relation to other colors, against black, against white, against gray. Overlapping or contiguous colors appear to be dimensionally different from those in isolation. The colors for this exercise were chosen for their harmonious relationship and have no symbolic significance.

Format:
26 x 36.6 centimeters.

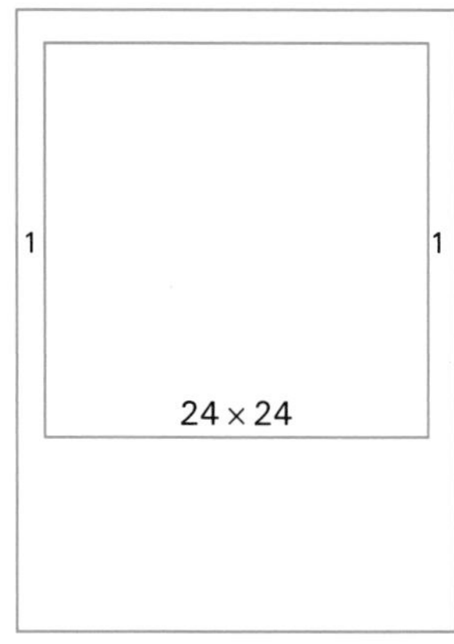

The format is based on a Root 2 rectangle, the proportion of which is derived from the square and its diagonal.
It is aesthetically pleasing and has certain practical advantages. Continuous folding in half yields the same proportion.
It is also the standard European paper proportion (DIN).

Materials:
3-ply kid finish bristol, colored papers, markers, tempera paints, or Plaka.

Bibliography

Léger, Douglas Cooper, Lund Humphries 1949
Léger, Katherine Kuh, University of Illinois 1953
Léger, Robert L. Delevoy, Skira 1962
Léger, Verdet, Sadea Sansoni 1969
Léger and Purist Paris, Tate Gallery 1970
Léger, Drawings and Gouaches, Cassou and Leymarie, New York Graphics Society 1973
Functions of Painting, Léger, Viking 1973
Léger, Werner Schmalenbach, Abrams 1976
Léger, Lawrence Saphire, Blue Moon Press 1978
1918, 1931: Léger and The Modern Spirit, G. Fabre, 1982
Léger and the Avant-Garde Christopher Green, Yale 1976
Fernand Léger Peter de Francia, Yale 1983

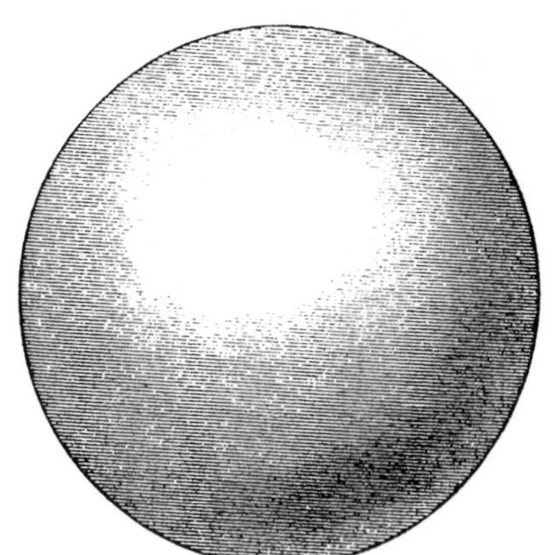

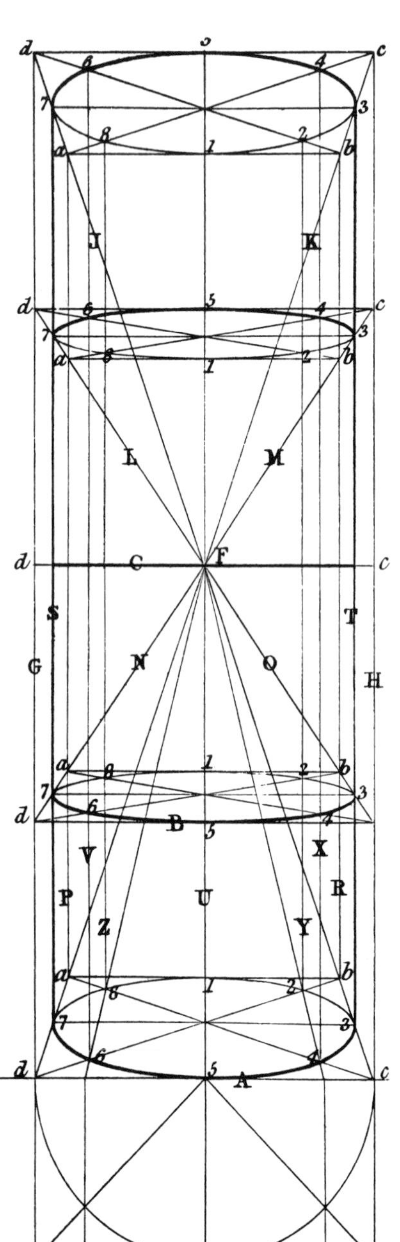
d 5 c
6 4
7 3
a 8 1 2 b
J K
d 6 5 4 c
7 3
a 8 1 2 b
L M
d C F c
S T
G N O H
a 8 1 2 b
7 3
d 6 B 5 4
V X
P U R
Z Y
a 8 1 2 b
7 3
d 6 5 A 4 c

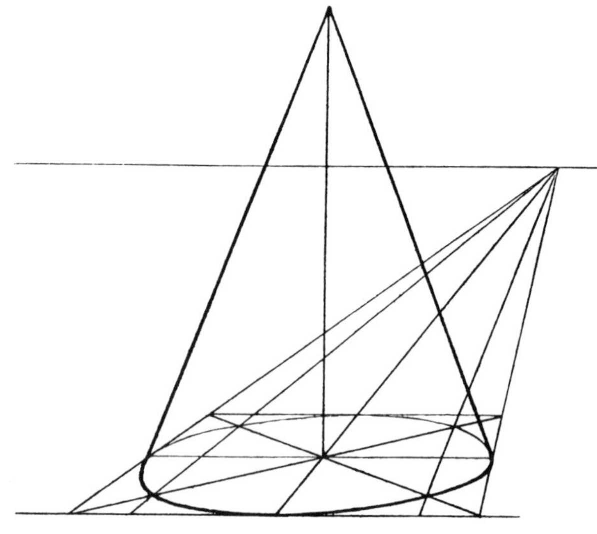

The lesson that we learn from Léger had its origins in Cézanne. As was the case with so many artists at the beginning of this century, however, it was a lesson Léger innocently misinterpreted.[1]

Theodore Reff, Cézanne and Poussin," *Journal of the Warburg and Courtauld Institute, Vol. 23* (London, 1960), 150-78.

On April 15, 1904, Cézanne, in a letter to Emil Bernard, wrote: "Treat nature by means of the cylinder, the sphere, and the cone, everything brought into proper perspective, so that each side of an object or a plane is directed towards a central point."[2] A simple lesson in Renaissance perspective was construed to mean that geometric simplicity would now play an important role in the way we perceive modern painting.

John Rewald, *Paul Cézanne Letters* (Oxford, 1976), 300.

This painting, made in 1913, clearly demonstrates that Léger took Cézanne's lesson quite literally. In Russia, at the same time, Kasimir Malevich, who was also very much influenced by Cézanne, painted pictures that were astonishingly similar to Léger's. Both disregarded the rules of perspective. Chiaroscuro was also used, but less as an indication of volume than as a means of creating interesting contrasts.

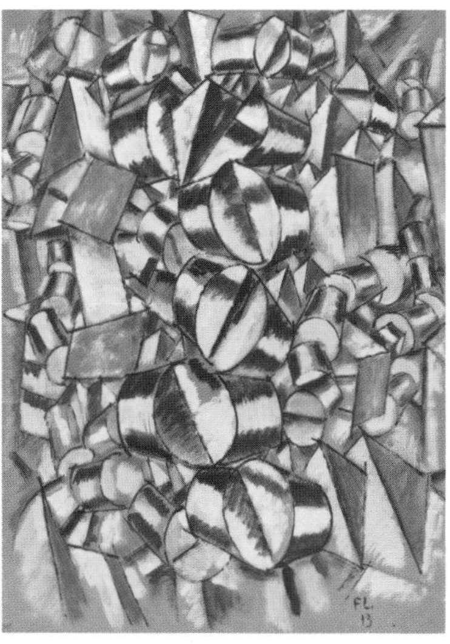

At the early part of the twentieth century, conscious of the changing views about art—Impressionism, Post Impressionism, Symbolism, Fauvism—the artist could quite easily have misread the real meaning of Cézanne's reference to the cylinder, the cone, and the sphere. In his enthusiasm he could easily have interpreted such a statement as heralding a new way of seeing. Ironically, what was new was not Cézanne's statement but the mistaken interpretation, which was, perhaps, most influential in changing the course of modern art and design in our time.

Paul Cézanne, Still Life with Apples, National Gallery of Art, Washington, D.C.

Fernand Léger, Contrast of Forms, 1913

Politics of Design

It is no secret that the real world in which the designer functions is not the world of art, but the world of buying and selling. For sales, and not design are the raison d'être of any business organization. Unlike the salesman, however, the designer's overriding motivation is art: art in the service of business, art that enhances the quality of life and deepens appreciation of the familiar world.

Design is a problem-solving activity. It provides a means of clarifying, synthesizing, and dramatizing a word, a picture, a product, or an event. A serious barrier to the realization of good design, however, are the layers of management inherent in any bureaucratic structure. For aside from sheer prejudice or simple unawareness, one is apt to encounter such absurdities as second-guessing, kow-towing, posturing, nit-picking, and jockeying for position, let alone such buck-passing institutions as the committee meeting and the task force. At issue, it seems, is neither malevolence nor stupidity, but human frailty.

The smooth functioning of the design process may be thwarted in other ways: by the imperceptive executive, who in matters of design understands neither his proper role nor that of the designer; by the eager but cautious advertising man whose principal concern is pleasing his client; and by the insecure client who depends on informal office surveys and pseudo-scentific research to deal with questions that are unanswerable and answers that are questionable.

Unless the design function in a business bureaucracy is so structured that direct access to the ultimate decision-maker is possible, trying to produce good work is very often an exercise in futility. Ignorance of the history and methodology of design—how work is conceived, produced, and reproduced—adds to the difficulties and misunderstandings. Design is a way of life, a point of view. It involves the whole complex of visual communication: talent, creative ability, manual skill, and technical knowledge. Aesthetics and economics, technology and psychology are intrinsically related to the process.

One of the more common problems which tends to create doubt and confusion is caused by the inexperienced and anxious executive who innocently expects, or even demands, to see not one but many solutions to a problem. These may include a number of visual and/or verbal concepts, an assortment of layouts, a variety of pictures and color schemes, as well as a choice of type styles. He needs the reassurance of numbers and the opportunity to exercise his personal preferences. He is also most likely to be the one to insist on endless revisions with unrealistic deadlines, adding to an already wasteful and time-consuming ritual. Theoretically, a great number of ideas assures a great number of choices, but such choices are essentially quantitative. This practice is as bewildering as it is wasteful. It discourages spontaneity, encourages indifference, and more often than not produces results which are neither distinguished, interesting, nor effective. In short, good ideas rarely come in bunches.

The designer who voluntarily presents his client with a batch of layouts does so not out of prolificacy, but out of uncertainty or fear. He thus encourages the client to assume the role of referee. In the event of genuine need, however, the skillful designer is able to produce a reasonable number of good ideas. But quantity by demand is quite different from quantity by choice. Design is a time-consuming occupation. Whatever his working habits, the designer fills many a wastebasket in order to produce one good idea. Advertising agencies can be especially guilty in this numbers game. Bent on impressing the client with their ardor, they present a welter of layouts, many of which are superficial interpretations of potentially good ideas, or slick renderings of trite ones.

Frequent job reassignments within an active business are additional impediments about which management is often unaware. Persons unqualified to make design judgments are frequently shifted into design-sensitive positions. The position of authority is then used as evidence of expertise. While most people will graciously accept and appreciate criticism when it comes from a knowledgeable source, they will resent it (openly or otherwise) when it derives solely from a power position, even though the manager may be highly intelligent or have self-professed "good taste." At issue is not the right, or even the duty, to question, but the right to make design judgment. Such misuse of privilege is a disservice to management and counterproductive to good design. Expertise in business administration, journalism, accounting, or selling, though necessary in its place, is not expertise in problems dealing with visual appearance. The salesman who can sell you the most sophisticated computer typesetting equipment is rarely one who appreciates fine typography or elegant proportions. Actually, the plethora of bad design that we see all around us can probably be attributed as much to good salesmanship as to bad taste.

Deeply concerned with every aspect of the production process, the designer must often contend with inexperienced production personnel and time-consuming purchasing procedures, which stifle enthusiasm, instinct, and creativity. Though peripherally involved in making aesthetic judgments (choosing printers, papermakers, typesetters, and other suppliers), purchasing agents are for the most part ignorant of design practices, insensitive to subtleties that mean quality, and unaware of marketing needs. Primarily and rightly concerned with cost-cutting, they mistakenly equate elegance with extravagance and parsimony with wise business judgment.

These problems are by no means confined to the bureaucratic corporation. Artists, writers, and others in the fields of communication and visual arts, in government or private industry, in schools or churches, must constantly cope with those who do not understand and are therefore unsympathetic to their ideas. The designer is especially vulnerable because design is grist for anybody's mill. "I know what I like" is all the authority one needs to support one's critical aspirations.

Like the businessman, the designer is amply supplied with his own frailties. But unlike him, he is often inarticulate, a serious problem in an area in which semantic difficulties so often arise. This is more pertinent in graphic design than in the industrial design or architectural fields, because graphic design is more open to aesthetic than to functional preferences.

Stubbornness may be one of the designer's admirable or notorious qualities (depending on one's point of view)—a principled refusal to compromise, or a means of camouflaging inadequacy. Design clichés, meaningless patterns, stylish illustrations, and predetermined solutions are signs of such weakness. An understanding of the significance of modernism and familiarity with the history of design, painting, architecture, and other disciplines, which distinguish the educated designer and make his role more meaningful, are not every designer's strong points.

The designer, however, needs all the support he can muster, for his is a unique but unenviable position. His work is subject to every imaginable interpretation and to every piddling piece of fault-finding. Ironically, he seeks not only the applause of the connoisseur, but the approbation of the crowd.

A salutary working relationship is not only possible but essential. Designers are not always intransigent, nor are all purchasing agents blind to quality. Many responsible advertising agencies are not unaware of the role that design plays as a communication force. As for the person who pays the piper, the businessman who is sympathetic and understanding is not altogether illusory. He is professional, objective, and alert to new ideas. He places responsibility where it belongs and does not feel insecure enough to see himself as an expert in a field other than his own. He is, moreover, able to provide a harmonious environment in which goodwill, understanding, spontaneity, and mutual trust – qualities so essential to the accomplishment of creative work – may flourish.

Similarly, the skilled graphic designer is a professional whose world is divided between lyricism and pragmatism. He is able to distinguish between trendiness and innovation, between obscurity and originality. He uses freedom of expression not as license for abstruse ideas, and tenacity not as bullheadedness but as evidence of his own convictions. His is an independent spirit guided more by an "inner artistic standard of excellence"[1] than by some external influence. At the same time as he realizes that good design must withstand the rigors of the marketplace, he believes that without good design the marketplace is a showcase of visual vulgarity.

1. Anthony Storr, *The Dynamics of Creation* (New York, 1972), 189.

The creative arts have always labored under adverse conditions. Subjectivity, emotion, and opinion seem to be concomitants of artistic questions. The layman feels insecure and awkward about making design judgments, even though he pretends to make them with a certain measure of know-how. But, like it or not, business conditions compel many to get inextricably involved with problems in which design plays some role.

For the most part, the creation or the effects of design, unlike science, are neither measurable nor predictable, nor are the results necessarily repeatable. If there is any assurance, besides faith, a businessman can have, it is in choosing talented, competent, and experienced designers.

Meaningful design, design of quality and wit, is no small achievement, even in an environment in which good design is understood, appreciated, and ardently accepted, and in which profit is not the only motive. At best, work that has any claim to distinction is the exception, even under the most ideal circumstances. After all, our epoch can boast of only one A. M. Cassandre.

Integrity and Invention

We are told "One picture is worth more than a thousand words," but is it? Does any one ad, poster, trademark, book jacket, letterhead, or TV commercial tell us of the compromises, doubts, frustrations, or misunderstandings that went into its making?

Some years ago I was asked to contribute a paper on the subject of the visual arts.[1] Those problems I chose to write about have, if anything, become even more apparent today than they were then. For the most part neither time, nostalgia, Victoriana, Art Deco, nor any other fashionable revival has warranted any substantial alterations in my views.

[1] *Daedalus* (Winter, 1960), 127-35.

Courage and Creativity

To function creatively the artist must have the courage to fight for what he believes. Courage in the face of a danger that has no element of high adventure in it – just the cold, hard possibility of losing his job. Yet the courage of his convictions is, along with his talent, his only source of strength. Frank Lloyd Wright put it this way:

I'll work as I'll think as I am
No thought of fashion or sham
Nor for fortune the jade
Serve vile Gods of trade
My thought as beseemeth a man[2]

[2] Frank Lloyd Wright, *Work Song* (Oak Book Workshop, 1896).

The businessman will never respect the professional who does not believe in what he does. The businessman under these circumstances can only use the artist for his own ends. And why not, if the artist himself has no ends? In asking the artist to have courage, we must ask the same of industry. The impetus to conform, so widespread today, will, if not checked, kill all forms of creativity, scientific and technological included.

Business has a strong tendency to wait for a few brave pioneers to produce or underwrite original work, then rushes to climb on the bandwagon. The bandwagon, of course, may not even be going in the right direction. The attention and admiration evoked by the high calibre of XYZ's advertising have induced many an advertiser to say, "Let's do something like XYZ" without considering that it might not be at all suited to his needs. Specific problems require specific visual solutions. But both XXX's and YYY's advertising and products can be made to fulfill their functions and also be aesthetically gratifying. Both can express respect for and concern with the broadest interests of the consumer.

Against the outstanding achievements in design by some companies, there stands the great dismal mountain of lacklustre work. On the whole, industry lacks confidence in creative talent and creative work, and this is the most serious obstacle to raising the standards of design.

Artistic Integrity

There are those who believe that the role the designer must play is fixed and determined by the socio-economic climate; that he must discover his functional niche and fit himself into it. It seems to me that this ready-made image ignores the part the artist can play in creating this climate. Whether we are advertising tycoons, missile builders, public figures, or private citizens, we are all human beings, and to endure we must, first of all, be *for* ourselves. Only when man is not accepted as the center of human concern does it become feasible to create a system of production which values profit out of proportion to responsible public service, or to design ads in which the only aesthetic criteria are the use of fashionable illustrations and "in" typefaces.

The Corporate Image

In this, the speed generation, practically any corporation, large or small, can have its "image" made to order. A vast army of image makers have made a business out of art large enough almost to rival the businesses they help to portray. Much has been touted about the virtues of corporate identification programs. Because the corporate image so often conveys the impression that it is all-encompassing, it leaves little doubt in the mind of the onlooker that the image he sees represents a company which is really in the swim; that it's the best, the first, and the most. However, being *with it* is not always being *for it.*

Upon receipt of the AIGA medal, for his company's contribution to good design, Irwin Miller, chairman of the executive committee of Cummins Engine Company, said: *"Good design has nothing to do with image, which is a phony word if there ever was one. Image is basically an attempt to cover up, a cosmetic applied to make you look better than you really do. Good design at heart is simply honesty. It is an ingredient of character. Good design helps to form in any one part of the business an influence that affects all parts of the business. It sustains character and honesty in every aspect of the business. Good design, therefore, is very good business indeed." (June 14, 1984)*

It seems to me that a company can more easily be recognized for what it really believes not by its made-to-order image (its trademark, logotype, letterhead), nor by the number of avant-garde prints or Mies van der Rohe chairs that embellish its offices, but by its more mundane, day-to-day activities: its house organs, counter displays, trade advertisements, packaging, and products. Unless it consistently represents the aims and beliefs as well as the total activity and production of a company, a corporate image is at best mere window dressing, and at worst deception.

Things can be made and marketed without considering their moral or aesthetic aspects; ads can convince without pleasing or heightening the spectator's visual awareness; products can work regardless of their appearance. But should they? The world of business could function without benefit of art. But should it? I think not, if only for the simple reason that the world would be a poorer place if it did.

The commercial artist (designer) who wants to be more than a mere stylist and who wishes to avoid being overwhelmed by the demands of clients, the idiosyncrasies of public taste, and the ambiguities of consumer research surveys must clarify what his cultural contribution should be. In all these areas he must try to distinguish the real from the imaginary, the sincere from the pretentious, and the objective from the biased.

If the graphic designer has both talent and a commitment to aesthetic values, he will automatically try to make the product of graphic design both pleasing and visually stimulating to the user or the viewer. By stimulating I mean that this work will add something to the spectator's experience.

The artist must believe his work is an aesthetic statement, but he must also understand his general role in society. It is this role that justifies his spending the client's money and his risking other people's jobs. And it entitles him to make mistakes. He adds something to the world. He gives it new ways of feeling and thinking. He opens doors to new experience. He provides new solutions to old problems.

There is nothing wrong with selling, even with "hard" selling, but selling which misrepresents, condescends, or relies on sheer gullibility or stupidity is wrong. Morally, it is very difficult for an artist to do a direct and creative job if dishonest claims are being made for the product he is asked to advertise, or if, as an industrial designer, he is supposed to exercise mere stylistic ingenuity to give an old product a new appearance. The artist's sense of worth depends on his feeling of integrity. If this is destroyed, he will no longer be able to function creatively.

Art and Communication

The lament of the graphic designer that he is not permitted to do good work because good work is neither wanted nor understood by his employers is universal. It is indeed very often true. But if the artist honestly evaluates his work he will frequently find that the "good work" the businessman has rejected is really not so good.

Many times when the "square" client says "it's too far out," he may be unconsciously reacting to inappropriate symbolism, obscure interpretation of an idea, poor typography, an inadequate display of his product, or simply bad communication.

Graphic design
which fulfills aesthetic needs,
complies with the laws of form and
the exigencies of two-dimensional space;
which speaks in semiotics, sans-serifs,
and geometrics;
which abstracts, transforms, translates,
rotates, dilates, repeats, mirrors,
groups, and regroups
is not good design if it is irrelevant.

Graphic design
which evokes the symmetria of Vitruvius,
the dynamic symmetry of Hambidge,
the asymmetry of Mondrian;
which is a good gestalt,
generated by intuition or by computer,
by invention or by a system of coordinates
is not good design
if it does not communicate.